As One Struggling Christian to Another

Theodore E. Tack, O.S.A.

As One Struggling Christian to Another

Augustine's Christian Ideal for Today

A Liturgical Press Book

THE LITURGICAL PRESS
Collegeville, Minnesota
www.litpress.org

Cover design by Greg Becker. Art: St. Augustine by Botticelli, Church of All Saints, Florence.

The author is grateful to the Augustinian Heritage Institute, Inc., Villanova, Pennsylvania, for permission to quote from *The Works of Saint Augustine* (all volumes), and *Spiritual Journey* by Cardinal Michele Pellegrino, © 1993 English translation of *The Works of Saint Augustine* and *Spiritual Journey,* Augustinian Heritage Institute, Inc.

The Scripture selections are taken from the New American Bible copyright © 1991, 1986, 1970 by the Confraternity of Christian Doctrine, 3211 Fourth Street, N.E., Washington, DC 20017-1194 and are used by license of the copyright owner. All rights reserved. No part of the New American Bible may be reproduced in any form or by any means without permission in writing from the copyright owner.

2	3	4	5	6	7	8

Library of Congress Cataloging-in-Publication Data

Tack, Theodore.
　　As one struggling Christian to another : Augustine's Christian ideal for today / Theodore E. Tack.
　　　　p. cm.
　　ISBN 0-8146-2415-4 (alk. paper)
　　1. Augustine, Saint, Bishop of Hippo. 2. Christian life–History–Early church, ca. 30–600. 3. Christian life–Catholic authors. I. Title.

BR65.A9 T3 2001
248.4–dc21

00-042847

Contents

Abbreviations

Sacred Scripture

All Scripture texts are from *The New American Bible.*

Texts of St. Augustine

Conf	*Confessions* [author's translation]
L	Letter
S	Sermon
Customs	*On the Customs of the Catholic Church . . .*
City	*The City of God*
On Ps	Commentary on Psalm
On John	Commentary on the Gospel of John
On 1 John	Commentary on the First Letter of John
Rule	The *Rule* of St. Augustine
Sol	*Soliloquies*

Other Works Cited

Bavel	Bavel, Tarsicius van, O.S.A. *The Rule of Saint Augustine. Introduction & Commentary.* Trans. R. Canning. London: Darton, Longman & Todd, 1984.
Catholic Bishops	*Economic Justice For All.* Pastoral letter on Catholic Social Teaching and the United States Economy. Washington,

	D.C.: National Conference of Catholic Bishops, 1986.
Corcoran	Corcoran, Gervase, O.S.A. *A Guide to the Confessions of St. Augustine*. Dublin: Carmelite Center, 1981.
Eastman	Eastman, Patrick. *"Monos"* 6 (1994) #4 [Private publication: Tulsa, Okla.]
Living	*Living in Freedom Under Grace*. Rome: Curia Generalizia Agostiniana, 1978.
Meer	Meer, Frederic van der. *Augustine the Bishop*. Trans. B. Battershaw and G. R. Lamb. London: Sheed and Ward, 1961.
Possidius	Possidius, Saint. *The Life of Saint Augustine*. Ed. John Rotelle, O.S.A. Villanova, Penn.: Augustinian Press, 1988.
Tack	Tack, Theodore, O.S.A. *If Augustine Were Alive*. New York: Alba House, 1988.
Trapè	Trapè, Agostino, O.S.A. *St. Augustine: Man, Pastor, Mystic*. Trans. Matthew J. O'Connell. New York: Catholic Book Publishing Co., 1986.

Preface

Most of us, if not all, find ourselves struggling every day with the challenges of the Christian life. But this is certainly nothing new. While the living of the Christian ideal brings great joy, it has also always been a challenge for those who have desired to take seriously the teachings of Jesus. The life and example of St. Augustine (354–430) offer remarkable insight into this challenge and the struggle to meet it. Augustine's very practical and pastoral approach to the Gospels has helped people grow in the Christian life down through the centuries. It has frankly amazed me to discover how relevant many of his thoughts and reflections are even for these times of great change in which we live.

Over the past several years, I have had many opportunities to speak about Augustine's approach to the Christian life to a number of high school and college-age students, as well as more mature adults. On several occasions I have also taught a course on Augustine's *Confessions*–his autobiographical masterpiece, which is one of the Great Books of all times. As a result of these experiences, I have been able to perceive that many people have been fascinated by these brief contacts with Augustine and have wanted to deepen their understanding of his spirituality. It is this interest which has encouraged me to make some of my reflections on Augustine's thought available to a larger audience through this book.

Experience has also taught me that many people today have a great desire to strengthen their faith by deepening the life of the Spirit within them. For not a few, this desire has been honed through the efforts of Pope John Paul II and other leaders of the Church, who have placed a great emphasis on a truly spiritual renewal for the third millennium. Over the years I have become convinced that Augustine's approach to the Scriptures and the Christian life can be of considerable help to others in reaching this goal of a deeper faith and a stronger interior life. But I am also convinced that Augustine's approach can be of great benefit for those who are struggling, just as he did, to maintain and grow in their faith, as well as for those who may have allowed the practice of their faith to drift.

On several occasions Augustine spoke to his people in these or similar words: "For you I am a bishop, but with you I am a Christian." These are striking lines in themselves, but his explanation of them is even more impressive. Here is one text:

> Though I am terrified by what I am for you, I am comforted by what I am with you. For you I am a bishop, but with you I am a Christian. The first is the name of an office I have accepted, the second is a grace. The first involves danger, the second salvation [S 340, 1].

Augustine knew that, in accepting to be a bishop, he had assumed a great responsibility before God for his people. He realized all too well the danger his episcopal duties imposed on him. However, this somewhat daunting realization in no way diminished his dedication to his people. Rather it made him more aware that he should continue to find his consolation, his comfort, and his strength in the initial gift that God had given him through his baptism in the Catholic Church. For him this following of Jesus Christ was the greatest grace, for it was the one that opened the way to salvation for him through membership in the Christian community.

Throughout his life Augustine sought to share with other men and women some of the gifts and insights God had shared with him. This book seeks to further that sharing, concerning itself with the reflections of this struggling Christian—Augustine—about the way of life proposed to us by Jesus of Nazareth, as it can be lived in our own times. While Augustine shares with others the great joy that comes from being a follower of Christ, he also makes clear the struggle that necessarily accompanies our striving to be faithful to that following. It was a struggle he knew only too well.

This book is not intended for scholars or experts. Their knowledge of Augustine goes far beyond anything I would have to offer here. Rather I am thinking principally of those who may wish to learn a little more about Augustine's reflections on the Christian life, so that they might grow in their faith and trust in God. In order to better understand Augustine's practical approach to this subject, I have attempted to supply the reader with some basic information about the man himself in the very first chapter. Augustine is frequently thought of as a great theologian and philosopher, and that he certainly is. But not many are aware of his deep spirituality, his appealing humanity, and the great struggle it cost him to discover and live the Christian life. Nor are many aware of his marvelous capacity to communicate his experiences in a vibrant and realistic way.

Other chapters in this book concern themselves with the basic challenges of the struggle to be a Christian: our common call to know better both ourselves and God, to be leaders in our world, to search for God and be intimate with him through prayer, to accept God's mercy through conversion, and to be Church—God's holy people—in the fullest sense of the word.

Two other chapters have been added concerning Augustine's relations with his people as their spiritual leader, and the pastoral problems anyone involved in ministry—priests, bishops, and others—might very well have to endure in leading others to Christ. I have added these chapters for two specific reasons: first, both the priesthood of the people and the priesthood of the ministry constitute an essential part of the Christian life. Second, these two chapters give special insights into some of the difficulties priests and pastors can experience in their service to others, difficulties that are good for all of us to be aware of. Furthermore, these difficulties and burdens are often common to all people who bear certain responsibilities for others.

On a few occasions I have used some of the thoughts and quotes from Augustine which appear in a book I published a few years ago, which concerned itself more with those who were living the consecrated Christian life in community (see *If Augustine Were Alive.* New York: Alba House, 1988). I have done this for the sake of continuity and cohesion, because Augustine's teaching on the Christian life is a composite. He himself frequently repeats ideas in his own writings and homilies.

I have touched on only a few aspects of the Christian life, aspects which I believe are among those fundamental to Augustine's spirituality. Other areas have already been considered in that other book of mine just mentioned. I sincerely hope that these few chapters will encourage readers to seek out still other books which offer Augustine's reflections, so that they may continue to grow in their ongoing search for God and in their love for his Son, Jesus Christ. Thankfully, many more such books are available today than even twenty or thirty years ago.

I wish to express profound gratitude to many of my brother Augustinians who have encouraged me in a variety of ways to continue deepening my knowledge of Augustine's spirituality and sharing it with others. A special word of gratitude is due to Mrs. Cathy Luccock, chair of the Cascia Hall School English Department, who accepted the demanding task of reading and critiquing this book. Her dedication to this task and her timely suggestions have greatly helped in making the text more readable and in enhancing its presentation.

I also gratefully acknowledge permission to use the English translation of *The Works of Saint Augustine* and *Spiritual Journey,* texts under the copyright of the Augustinian Heritage Institute, Inc.

1

A Man for Our Times

Legends abound when it comes to great historical figures, and St. Augustine's life presents no exception to this norm. One of the legends told about him has been firmly fixed in paint by medieval artists. The painting shows a stately Augustine, mitered and dressed in bishop's attire with cope and stole, bending over a small child who, with a play shovel, is digging a hole in the sand on an otherwise deserted beach. Some people might question why Augustine would have gone to the beach in such formal attire, but that particular problem probably never entered the artist's mind. No, the artist was only interested in portraying a legend, no matter the scenery, so Augustine had to be there as bishop and teacher of the Church.

Now here is the legendary story behind this painting: Augustine is bending down to the child and asking him what he is doing. To which this tiny tyke responds: "I'm digging a hole in the sand so I can put the ocean in it." At this, Augustine supposedly smiled down at the little boy and told him that what he was trying to do was impossible. To which our young lad is said to have replied: "Well, it's just as impossible for you or any other person, with your limited minds, to try to explain the mystery of the Blessed Trinity!" Wow! Out of the mouths of children, *Wisdom!* Or as the legend has it: out of the mouth of an angel in the form of a child, an important message for Augustine as he began to write his book on the Blessed Trinity.

Whether this or anything similar ever really happened we will never know. Augustine himself tells us nothing about it, and he tended to relate his experiences very candidly, even when they did not flatter him. But what we do know is that he did write a lengthy volume on the mystery of the Blessed Trinity, and though he succeeded in casting light on some things through similarities with what our human experience teaches us, at the end of the book the Trinity still remained a mystery of faith, just as it continues to be to this day, sixteen centuries later.

I tell you this little story for a special reason. Augustine himself is a topic as broad and as deep as the ocean itself. How does one do justice to the vital role Augustine has played and still plays in the life of the Church in a short book like this, or even in a longer one? That would be very much like trying to fit the ocean into a child's hole in the sand. Thousands of books and articles have been written about Augustine in the twentieth century alone, and yet the topic—Augustine, his writings, or both—never seems to be exhausted. I gladly admit to being an amateur when it comes to knowledge of Augustine's writings, but I am a very enthusiastic amateur. I have a truly great love and esteem for him as a human being, a dedicated Christian, and a leader of the Church, who is at the same time the spiritual Father of the Augustinians, a religious Order founded in the thirteenth century to follow Augustine's religious ideal. As Augustine is a great source of inspiration for those who imitate his special way of following Christ, so is he also an inspiration for many other Christians today, just as he has been through the centuries. Perhaps some facts and figures will help us understand this a little better.

Some Facts and Figures

From the time of his conversion at almost age thirty-two until his death forty-four years later, Augustine wrote over one hundred books, some of them of quite astounding length. As a priest and bishop, he constantly preached to the people, certainly every Sunday and often on weekdays. About six hundred of these homilies have been preserved, and more are being found almost every year among the dusty manuscripts of some libraries of Europe. Despite the fact that sending letters in the days in which he lived (354–430 C.E.) was a very risky business (there was no real postal system as we have today, and no one ever knew exactly when and if the letter would arrive!), over 270 of Augustine's letters have survived to our times. The person who wants to do research on Augustine is in for a truly formidable, but rich experience.

In 1986, the Church commemorated the 1600th anniversary of Augustine's conversion to the Catholic faith. Pope John Paul II himself published a special Apostolic Letter for the occasion, in which he very briefly outlined some of Augustine's extensive contributions to the Church. Augustine's conversion took place in Milan, Italy, in late July or early August of the year 386; his baptism followed in the cathedral church of Milan during the Easter Vigil the following year, on April 24–25, 387. He was baptized by another great saint of the Church, Ambrose, who had been instrumental in bringing about Augustine's conversion.

The Church has never forgotten Augustine's philosophical and theological contribution to structuring the faith. In fact he has been called a second St. Paul because of what he gave the Church. Pope Paul VI, of happy memory, constantly quoted Augustine in many of his speeches and writings. He was enamored of this spiritual giant, whose teaching on the Christian life is, as Pope Paul puts it, "unique for its richness, unique for its clarity of thought, unique for its depth of human experience, unique for its modernity" [Living 47].

But above all, Vatican Council II, which was principally a pastoral Council as the bishops themselves have told us, called on Augustine's wisdom in many ways to confirm its own teaching, precisely because Augustine was such a pastoral person himself. He is by far the most quoted author in the documents of that Council, and oftentimes he is paraphrased when he is not directly quoted. It is as though the Council were telling us that, though we are living in an entirely new age, this age has very definite Augustinian characteristics. For example, ours is an age in which the Church has sought to draw more closely together the City of God and the City of the World, just as Augustine did. Ours too is an age which seeks to emphasize both individuality and community, as well as Christian action and contemplation, or interior prayer. In all this, we find ever so much of Augustine, who sought to live a balanced existence himself and to encourage others—married, single, religious, or clergy—to live the Christian life in a similar way. This simply means we should never let ourselves lose sight of the individual's needs, nor allow the individual to lose sight of being a part of the community or family. We recognize the need to make our faith practical through an active love, without losing sight of the need to build up our interior prayer life with God.

My purpose in presenting these statistics and facts about Augustine has not been done with any desire to overawe but rather to put Augustine in a modern-day perspective. Down through the centuries he has been both highly praised and severely criticized for some of his theological statements and stands. But what his critics have often failed to note is the context in which he wrote, the times that were his, the unstructured and unresearched nature of Catholic theology in his day. Augustine never attempted to structure theological studies in any way, much less as we know them today. But his wealth of reflection on the Scriptures and on the great mysteries of our faith laid a firm foundation for those who were to come after him. Unfortunately, he has been misunderstood and misinterpreted, just as the Scriptures themselves.

On the other hand, some, both within the Church and outside it, have almost attributed to Augustine a quasi-infallibility, something he never pretended for himself in any way, and which would be totally unfitting for any individual bishop, outside of the pope in very special circumstances. However, since the purpose of this book is not to delve into his opinions on theological or philosophical matters, I would like to address some other facets of this extraordinary man's life. I think these will help illustrate how down to earth he was and how remarkably relevant he has been for people of all generations and continues to be for us, who live in times which in many ways resemble his own.

But first, let me very briefly give you some background information on Augustine's first thirty-something years before his conversion. This will help put in perspective what follows.

Early Life

Augustine was born on November 13, 354, in the small town of Thagaste (modern-day Souk-Ahras) in a region then known as Numidia (now Algeria), a dependency of the Roman Empire in northern Africa. His mother Monica was of the Berber tribe, a Bedouin group in that area. His father Patrick came from a long-standing Roman family in the town: he was well respected, though of modest financial means. Monica was a Catholic, but Patrick had no particular religious beliefs.

Augustine was raised a Catholic, growing to love the name of Jesus, as he learned it from infancy on his mother's lap. However, contrary to practice in other parts of the Church, he was not baptized as an infant. When he was fifteen he spent a year in idleness at home, while his father did all he could to raise money to send his promising son to the very best university of the region, which was located some two hundred miles away in Carthage (near present-day Tunis, in Tunisia). When Augustine finally arrived at the university in his seventeenth year, his father had died, but not before being baptized in the Catholic faith.

During that year of idleness in Thagaste, however, Augustine began a spiral of descent into sin and away from the faith of his youth, which became much more pronounced once he reached the university. He himself describes this situation far better than we could: "During my adolescence I burned with desire for an abundance of the basest things possible. I dared to run wild, seeking many-faceted and dark ways of loving . . . My heart was unable to distinguish the unclouded light of love from the blackness of lust" [Conf 2, 1–2].

While at the university in Carthage, he began living with a young girl, by whom he had a child, Adeodatus. Augustine was eighteen at the time. He joined a popular religious sect called the Manichees, which proclaimed that there were two gods, one of light and one of darkness, who were constantly in conflict with one another. Despite his keen intellectual ability, Augustine was taken in by this group because they promised him an answer to two concerns in particular that really bothered him: the problem of evil and the problem of the nature of God as a pure spirit. Furthermore, what really won him over was their assurance that they could answer all his problems by the light of pure reason.

Augustine remained with this sect for over nine years, finally leaving them when he was convinced they could not help him as they had promised. Then he started drifting toward believing in astronomers, dabbling in the various philosophies of the day, especially the neo-Platonists, and even reconsidering what the Catholic Church was teaching.

Two major influences in these early years of manhood were his mother, Monica, and Ambrose, the saintly bishop of Milan (the city where Augustine had begun teaching in his thirty-first year). Although Monica was very much opposed to Augustine's belonging to the Manichees, she stood by her errant son. And though Augustine did not always agree with her, he had the greatest love and esteem for her. Ambrose appealed to Augustine because he was a "rhetorician"—a master of words and speech—like Augustine, and a very skilled speaker at that. Augustine loved to listen to him preach because he was fascinated by his style, but as he listened, he also, quite involuntarily, began to take in what Ambrose was saying about the Catholic faith.

Within two years, Augustine's restless search for the truth reached its climax. He could no longer find happiness by dabbling in various philosophies, though the neo-Platonists did help him understand how a purely spiritual god could exist. Several circumstances came together to bring about his actual conversion to the faith, which he describes in a very powerful scene in his autobiography, *Confessions*. We shall be reflecting on this scene in detail in chapter 4.

As already noted, his conversion took place in the summer of 386. Augustine was not yet thirty-two. Shortly after his baptism in the year 387, he returned to his home town of

Thagaste. Eventually he was chosen to be a priest and bishop of nearby Hippo, a large coastal city, which is now known as Annaba in Algeria.

Augustine's Confessions

How is it we know so much about this man who lived sixteen centuries ago? Mainly because he has told us about himself in his book *Confessions,* just mentioned above. The title of that book is certainly misleading for our times: it is no racy account of sex and lust such as we might find in some magazines. It is, however, a very honest and humble account of those early years of his life, which I have just briefly spoken of, when he had strayed far from the Church and was motivated by an ever growing passion for wealth, prestige, and women. It also gives us keen insights into Augustine's character.

The *Confessions* has been reading material for Christians and non-Christians alike since it was first written between 397–401, when Augustine was in the prime of his life, forty-three to forty-seven years old. It is one of the recognized Great Books of all time, and, more than other Great Books, is also still widely read. Good translations of this book exist in almost every major language. There are some excellent paperback editions available in English, and even very recent new translations. It is possibly one of the most widely-circulated and widely-read books that was ever written.

What is the real appeal of this book? Personally, I believe it is the appeal of the man who wrote it. Without having studied modern psychology, he gives us extraordinary psychological insights into ourselves. His personal odyssey, his fall from the Church and into sin and a non-Christian sect at age eighteen; his pride, passion, and search for honors; his gradual recognition of the fact that he was not happy, though he had many earthly blessings and an assured economic future; his return to the faith—all these things, plus his great thirst for God and the difficulties he experienced in finding and holding on to God, relate to a basic human need and strike an empathetic chord in all who would be honest with themselves, today and always.

Augustine's Times and Our Times

Interestingly enough, the problems Augustine had to face in his own day were quite similar to some we must face. His were times of great social upheaval: the old Roman Empire, which had been around for some six centuries, was crumbling all around him. There was strong change in the wind, and no one could see where it would lead or when things would settle down again. Does that sound familiar? How much social, political, professional, religious, legal, and personal change have we seen, especially since the 1960s? But in the midst of all that uncertainty, Augustine was not afraid of change, and that should be encouraging to us also who live in this third Christian millennium. Listen to how he encouraged his own people not to get stuck in a rut, but to keep moving at all times:

> You see, we are on a journey. Never stop questioning yourself . . . Let your present state always leave you dissatisfied if you want to become what you are not yet. For whenever you find yourself satisfied, you stop making progress. If you say: "That's enough!", you are lost. You must always add something more, keep moving forward, make progress. Do not halt along the way, do not turn back. Above all do not leave the beaten path. It would be better for you to limp along the right road, than to find yourself running in the wrong direction [S 169, 18].

Augustine also had some very keen insights into the Christian life itself. What he emphasized in his sermons are the very points which many people tend to emphasize today. For example: (1) Augustine strongly promoted a deep sense of Christian community; (2) he affirmed a common search for and praise of God; (3) he saw genuine friendship as one of the most important blessings of life; (4) he reflected true respect for the individual, even while the common good was to be defended; (5) he encouraged his people to a deeply interior life and a restless pursuit of wisdom and truth. Through this pursuit he was convinced they would find God; (6) above all, he wanted them to find and serve Christ in one another through a wholly practical, mutual service and love;

(7) he constantly accented the dignity and intrinsic value of the human person within the social environment, a theme which is very much stressed in our own day and age, and perhaps especially by Pope John Paul II.

A few years ago when I was speaking to a large gathering of Catholic laity in Chicago, I used a quotation from Augustine which is so modern that they could not believe it had been written sixteen centuries earlier. Augustine had addressed it to those who were always complaining that things seemed so bad in their times, so bad that they wanted to return to the past, because then life had certainly been better. "Don't kid yourself," Augustine tells them, though he does say this in more diplomatic terms:

> We should not grumble, my brothers and sisters . . . Is there any affliction now endured by mankind that was not endured by our ancestors before us? . . . And yet you hear people complaining about this present day and age because things were so much better in former times. I wonder what would happen if they could be taken back to the days of those ancestors—would we not still hear them complaining? You may think past ages were good, but it is only because you are not living in them . . . Far from justifying complaints about our own time, they teach us how much we have to be thankful for [S 346C, 1].

Some Common Areas of Concern

What did Augustine know about the problems of our times? What did he know about terrorism, for example, or drugs, or disunity in the Church? Believe it or not, he knew a lot about these topics, which are so real for us. Some of us seem to believe that terrorism is something new to our age. Wrong! It has been around for a long time. Augustine knew at first hand the violence that is terrorism, as well as the way it preyed on his clergy and people. By a strange quirk of fate—and by the workings of Providence!—the driver of his carriage took a detour one day while driving Augustine home. In so doing he saved the good bishop from being set upon by some terrorists who had been lying in wait to beat him up. On other occasions some of his clergy were not so fortunate:

some were beaten, one was killed, others had their houses burned. It was not easy living in those days [see Possidius 12].

There were drugs too—maybe not the kind we know, but powerful drugs just the same. The drugs of his time were the strong, emotional impact of the spectacles arranged for entertainment by the State: the bloody fights of the gladiators in the arena and the sensuous drama of the theater. Augustine, the youth, and thousands of others like him had fallen victim to this drug addiction to the extent that they were powerfully drawn to witness these spectacles and have their passions aroused by the violence and suggestive nature of the scenes they observed. Violence and pornography were as prevalent then as now.

And disunity in the Church? Well, in 396 when Augustine took over as bishop in the Mediterranean seaport city of Hippo, he was a minority bishop. A break-away sect of North African Catholics, known as the Donatists, dominated this city and many others around it. Interestingly enough, the Donatists claimed to be the only true Christians and persecuted others who would not join them or, worse, who would dare leave their sect. I wonder if we have not seen similar dissension in our own days? The late Archbishop Lefevbre separated from the Church after Vatican II, defying the patient and loving authority of two popes, who for so long tried to bring him and his followers back to unity. The good archbishop claimed loyalty to a pope also, but it was to one who had died four centuries earlier. He would not allow for any change whatsoever even in externals, which have nothing to do with the truths the Church has taught and defended without change down through the centuries.

Speaking of these Donatists reminds me of one of the first truths I learned as a small child in catechism class: that no matter how bad a priest or bishop might be in his personal life, the sacraments he administered were not tainted nor without their grace-filled effect if a minister acted in the manner prescribed by the Church. And the reason was very simple: priests and bishops do not own the sacraments. They are a gift of Christ, and the grace comes from Christ himself, not from the minister. Little did I know at that time that this was the very teaching used by Augustine to save the Church from the error of the Donatists in his own day. These Donatists had said, in effect, that the bishops who had allowed the sacred books to be burned in the time of persecution were not worthy to pass on the priesthood or the bishop's office to others: they were tainted and impure, and any sacrament they administered was ineffective, invalid.

The Spiritual Life of the Christian

Augustine was an expert teacher of the spiritual life for his people. Much of what he said to them is also relevant for us in this new millennium. How can this be? Principally because Augustine well understood human nature and how to direct that nature toward what alone would bring it true happiness and peace: that is, the possession of God. In that most famous line by which he is known, Augustine sums up in very succinct words a yearning that we all experience: "You have made us for yourself, Lord, and our heart is restless until it rests in you" [Conf 1, 1]. Really what that line says in its original form is that we have been made to "journey toward" God, and we can never experience true peace until that journey is completed and we have arrived.

This very ingrained restlessness, placed within us by our Creator, is the real driving force that keeps honest people searching for God, no matter what the obstacles they run into. Our restless journey is a lifelong love affair with God, but one that fills us over and over again with happiness along the way.

The greatest personal discovery that Augustine made during his fifteen-year absence from the Church as a youth and his relentless pursuit of the truth was that God was not far from him. In fact, he discovered that God was closer to him than he was to himself: "You were more intimate to me than my deepest being . . ." [Conf 3, 6]. Augustine had wandered far afield searching for God without realizing this intimacy. But when he did come to this awareness, God touched Augustine's heart and indeed all his senses, as God often does for us also. Augustine sums up this experience in these striking words:

You called to me and your cry shattered my deafness. You blazed forth and your splendor put my blindness to flight. You poured out your fragrance and I drew in my breath and now I pant after you. I tasted you and I hunger and thirst after you. You touched me, and I have burned with a desire for your peace [Conf 10, 27].

Augustine urges all of us to become more aware of the great gift which we carry within ourselves: the presence of God. But he also urges us to do something with this gift. Do not let it just be a nice feeling, he says. Rather, let it move you to a very practical, outgoing faith.

In this vein, a few years ago our American Catholic bishops published a very challenging pastoral letter on "Economic Justice For All," a letter which concerned itself with Catholic social teaching and the United States economy. Early on in this letter the bishops state very clearly: "No one may claim the name Christian and be comfortable in the face of the hunger, homelessness, insecurity, and injustice found in this country and the world" [#27]. This was also one of Augustine's favorite topics, as he tried to move his people to appreciate that the poor, the oppressed, and the needy were Christ himself, still suffering here on earth.

Bishop Augustine frequently reminded his people that there were indeed two commandments of love laid upon us by the Scriptures: love of God and love of neighbor. Love of God is certainly the greater of these two commandments, he says. But in the same breath he adds that if you really want to love God, you have to begin by loving your neighbor. There is no way you can prove your love for God, except by showing your love for those around you in a very practical way. It is easy enough to profess love for God or another person. It is quite a different story to show this love in a practical, concrete way. And that is exactly the same challenge that our bishops and our Holy Father the pope call us to in our own times.

Augustine is truly a man for our times, a teacher who still has much to say to those who will listen to him. His Christian ideal is vibrant and very modern. And though he certainly does not have an answer for all the complicated problems of our times, there is great wisdom and psychological penetration in his thought, which encourages those who read him and challenges them to search restlessly and without ceasing for their God.

The chapters that follow will attempt to present more in depth some of Augustine's thoughts on several of the above-mentioned topics and others which affect the daily living of our Christian life.

2

Identity Crises: The Need to Know Ourselves and God

I have been teaching ethics to high school seniors for many years now. On the whole it has been a very rewarding experience. At the end of each course I have been able to see that many of my students have acquired a broader view, both of life and of several of the burning issues associated with life today. How satisfying it has been to have some of them comment in writing that the course made them think more deeply, reason out issues more clearly, even at times change their views from pro-choice to pro-life, understand better some of the life-death decisions made in their own families about withholding treatment from a very sick relative because that treatment was really ineffective.

Searching for Happiness

Every time I begin that ethics course with a new and eager group of students, one of the first questions I confront them with is this: What is it that every one of us is seeking in every activity that we undertake? Now that's quite a question for a teenager, even for a senior. For a few minutes, I receive all kinds of answers: we are seeking money, love, prestige, and the like. No, I tell them. That's not what's behind it! Then invariably one or two of them come up with the right answer: happiness. Yes, that's exactly the answer. Happiness is what we all constantly seek, no matter what we are doing, good or bad.

But the big question is, how do we achieve this happiness? Do we actually find it as a result of everything we do? Experience answers: Not at all. Well, at least not in the manner in which we are really searching for it. The happiness we are really searching for is a lasting happiness, one that can never be taken away from us. Augustine pinned down that answer when he wrote at the beginning of his *Confessions* that we have an innate restlessness that can never be satisfied until we possess God [see Conf 1, 1]. What a tremendous amount of truth in that thought! Our hearts simply cannot be happy until they are filled with God. That's the way it is, because that's the way we have been made by a loving God who wants us to be totally happy and self-fulfilled in the truest sense of the word. Yet often it takes people a lifetime to discover the meaning of all this for themselves. It took Augustine a good fifteen years to come to that realization and do something about it. I wonder how much it affects you and me today?

Augustine prayed for knowledge of himself, but he always did so while seeking knowledge of God. As he wrote: "Let me know myself, let me know you!" [Sol 1]. He prayed that he might know himself first, and *then* know God. Some would say he had it backwards. Should we not first seek to know God, and then ourselves? The answer is really similar to what St. John the Evangelist says about loving God: You can't love God whom you do not see, if you do not first love your neighbor whom you do see [see 1 John 4:20]. Along the same lines, how can we say that we know God, whom we do not see, if we do not know ourselves, or understand who we are and where we are headed, though we literally live with ourselves day in and day out?

Identity Crises

When we were younger, could we ever have imagined that priests and religious could have identity crises? Before Vatican II it might have been quite difficult for most Christians to think that way. Since then, however, the very human side of priests and religious has been brought much more sharply to the fore. We have seen up close some of these unfortunate failings, and they have been very painful to all. Yet at the same time this may have also made it easier to recognize and acknowledge more of the many good points of others. Jesus too was the object of much adverse criticism in his own lifetime. And in the course of history, when his humanity or divinity was over-emphasized or downplayed, his role as our Savior was obscured or lost. The best images we have of Jesus are those that have emphasized both his humanity and divinity. We may find it much easier to relate to the human Jesus, but we also find ourselves strengthened and encouraged because he is at the same time our God.

Vatican II asked all religious to go back to their roots, to rediscover what they were supposed to be by examining the very beginnings of their existence. In this way all were challenged to take a deeper look at themselves, to recognize their identity anew, because the bishops of the Council were convinced that this would be of the greatest benefit to the entire Church. You know, they were right! I can speak from some experience about my religious order, the Augustinians. We put ourselves through much self-scrutiny in those years immediately following the Council, but as a result we were able to find our way back to a clearer and more accurate view of Augustine's ideal of religious life and that of our healthy tradition. We discovered that we needed to emphasize a few matters much more than we had in the past, and at the same time to rid ourselves of some practices that were no longer meaningful to our life in the Order.

But identity crises are by no means limited to priests or religious. All God's people can suffer identity crises because they have never really learned to know themselves. And that is a great shame, because if we cannot know ourselves, how can we ever hope to truly know others, including God? Knowing ourselves is like getting to the bottom of a mystery. It is to finally understand and appreciate who we are, our very positive points, as well as those that are not so pleasant. A few years ago a college teacher I know wrote a book which she uses to teach her students how to discover the mystery of their own life story through writing. It has proved a very useful tool for those who have had her as their teacher in the classroom. Knowing ourselves, getting to the bottom of this "mystery," which we frequently are to ourselves, is really the only way we can strengthen what is positive and good about us and at the same time correct our failings and mistakes. It would be tragic not to learn from our mistakes and failings.

Helpful Insights from Augustine

It is comforting to know that others before us have faced the same identity crises and have come through with flying colors, though not without some real pain and suffering. St. Augustine was a perfect example of this. In his *Confessions* he lets us see himself in a very human way: that is, we see his good points, along with those negative characteristics that nearly destroyed him. At times he paints a very dismal and perhaps exaggerated picture of himself. Yet it is still quite an authentic image of how he saw himself as he looked back over the years. What he sees and often quite remarkably describes frequently turns out to be a striking reflection of our own personal experience or that of someone near or dear to us. His reflections can and do help us see ourselves more clearly and appreciate all the more who we are.

For example, Augustine the bishop was struck by the fact that people seemed very interested in going to great lengths to view the marvels of nature, yet strangely enough they did not know themselves! This is how he put it:

> Quite frankly I do not understand all that I am . . . and I cannot help but be filled with wonder and even fear at this. Yet people travel far and wide and are astonished at the height of the mountains, the huge waves of the sea, the rushing currents of the rivers, the vast expanse of the ocean, or the rotation of the stars. But they pay no attention to themselves [Conf 10, 8].

What Augustine noted in his own time, we can still see in ours. There are many people in the world today who are keenly aware of how to handle business matters or be successful in other areas of life. And yet, at the same time, they do not seem to have a grasp on what the real purpose of life might be. In other words, they do not understand themselves and why they exist. Some, as we also know, even bombard their minds with constant distractions, precisely because they fear having to face themselves.

Augustine reveals his own ignorance of himself specifically in those passages where he speaks about how he was searching for God—and failing to find him.

> But where was I when I was searching for you? You were there before my eyes, but I had wandered away from myself. I could not find myself, and much less could I find you [Conf 5, 2].

> Late have I loved you, Beauty at once so ancient and so new! Late have I loved you! You were within me, and I was outside myself. And it was outside myself that I searched for you. Unsightly as I was, I threw myself upon the lovely things of your creation. You were with me, but I was not with you [Conf 10, 27].

What Augustine experienced is common enough in our own times. Many are so taken up with the material world around them, or so distracted with such things as soap operas, talk shows, loud music, sensual attractions, or constant movement, that they simply do not find time for anything else—neither for God, nor for themselves. They fail to see their own very evident weaknesses!

How God Knows Us

But while we seek to know ourselves and to know God, it is interesting to reflect on how God knows us. A quick look at the prophets of the Old Testament can help us greatly in this regard.

The call of the great prophets of biblical times—Samuel, Elisha, Isaiah, Jeremiah, Ezekiel, and others—has always fascinated me. But Jeremiah's call is the one that has always struck a particular chord in my heart, because Jeremiah seemed to be more aware than many others of what was going to be expected of him if he were to say "yes" to the Lord's invitation or call. Consequently, because he foresaw some very difficult and challenging situations, he experienced real fear, as most of us would, and he showed it in his response to that call.

> The word of the LORD came to me thus:
> Before I formed you in the womb I knew you,
>> before you were born I dedicated you,
>> a prophet to the nations I appointed you.
> "Ah, LORD GOD," I said,
>> "I know not how to speak; I am too young."
> But the LORD answered me,
> Say not, "I am too young."
>> To whomever I send you, you shall go;
>> whatever I command you, you shall speak.
> Have no fear before them,
>> because I am with you to deliver you," says the LORD
>> [Jer 1:4-8].

This text can apply not just to prophets or priests, but to all of us. God has truly known us from the moment we were conceived in our mother's womb, and from that time he has called us to be who we are and, in Augustine's words, to become what "we are not yet" [see S 169, 18]. God has allowed us to be born into a world that is terribly secular and terribly godless, because it is so frequently wrapped up in itself and in material pursuits that it has neglected its Creator. God has asked us to be in the world, without allowing ourselves to be overcome by the world's materialistic views. We are to be witnesses to his existence, to his glory, to his kingdom, to a reality totally different from that touted by media programs and advertisements, and to do this by the very way we live our Christian lives. Above all, he has told us not to fear, something that John Paul II has reiterated frequently in his writings and speeches.

God told Jeremiah not to fear because he would be with him to deliver him. In the same fashion Jesus has told us he will be with us all days, even to the very end of the world. Neither God nor Jesus, however, ever promised to save the prophets or ourselves from temptation, pain, suffering, mis-understanding, persecution, or death. In other words, God will not save us from our humanity. But being with us, God and Jesus have promised to "deliver us," give us, that is, the strength to be faithful, to be fully ourselves, and not to be done in by the powers of evil.

A Very Personal Relationship

These are consoling thoughts, but they also go much fur-ther than merely consoling us. They point out the very close, personal relationship that God has always established with his chosen people, that Jesus taught personally in his own time, and which he now continues to communicate to us through the gospel and the sacraments.

Yet not all, perhaps not even the majority of people, are sufficiently aware of this very personal relationship that God has established with his people and desires that we recipro-cate. How could we ever reciprocate if we did not first of all come to know God, love him, and finally grow to be his friends? Therein is a true mutual relationship: love demand-ing a like response. Yet, as I was saying, there are all too many who are insufficiently aware of God's desires, or, if they are aware of them, they seem to ignore them blithely by the way they live. How does God reach them? How does God get through to you and me? How does God communi-cate to us a better understanding and feeling for what this personal relationship really means, both to God and to us? Augustine put it to his people in very clear language:

> God made you . . . in his own image. Would he give you an eye to see the sun he created and not give you an eye to see him who made you, even after making you in his own like-ness? No, he gave you such an eye. In fact, he gave you both kinds of eyes. Yet you greatly esteem these outer eyes, and sorely neglect the eye within [S 88, 6].

For Augustine the *eye within* is the light of eternal wis-dom which God has placed in our minds and hearts to help us know him. But Augustine also discovered how this seem-ingly abstract inner light of wisdom shows itself in a very human way through the interior restlessness we all experience: *our hearts are restless until they rest in you.* That is, we come to know God through our very human nature, which is always searching for a happiness that will last.

God will not let us be satisfied with mere passing things, with anything less than himself. He has given us an inner drive by which we constantly search for what will make us totally happy—and we often go wide of the mark in our search. Many beautiful things of creation, many beautiful people, attract and partially fill us. And the more we give ourselves over to them, without setting proper priorities for ourselves, the more easily can they distract us, turn us away, and perhaps even succeed in blocking out what alone can truly satisfy these inmost longings of our nature.

A Restless Journey Toward God

All of us, just like Augustine, are on a restless journey. And this is true even though we are already aware of God's presence in our lives, aware of the Christian call we have received, and possessed by a deep desire to know and love God ever better. The reason is very simple: we can never know God sufficiently, either in this life or in the next, because God is without limits, boundless, so to speak. Yet while God is infinite, without limits, we are finite and very limited.

Many years ago a lady came to me seeking counsel. She was very upset at the thought of how boring heaven would be if it would mean we were just staring at God all day long! That is like the old idea of heaven being a place where we all play harps! I must admit, I too would be bored by such a scenario. We do not have any scriptural explanation of heaven, but by the very fact that God is infinite and we are finite, it will be a constantly new experience: we will always be understanding and enjoying new aspects of God's life, beauty, love, and relationships. A very human and inadequate parallel to this could be given by referring to what I have experienced when traveling between Italy and Switzerland by train. The scenery is constantly changing: towering mountains and lush green valleys are punctuated by streams and waterfalls, by picturesque villages; the same scene is viewed from different perspectives, from great heights or from lowly meadows, and from in-between heights, too. Of course, since none of us has yet had that divine experience of being with God in heaven and returning to talk about it, we must take it on faith: "Eye has not seen, and ear has not heard, nor has it so much as dawned on man what God has prepared for those who love him" [1 Cor 2:9]. That is St. Paul quoting Isaiah 64:3. Certainly God knows best what will completely satisfy our deepest longings for happiness. Augustine explained it to his people this way:

> God fills the one who seeks him, insofar as that person's capacity permits; and he increases that capacity in the one who finds him, so that this person might again seek to be filled . . . Let us never cease to make progress along this way, until it brings us to our goal, where we can remain forever . . . [On John 63, 1].

This challenge to keep moving and keep growing is very much in line with the "restlessness," that dynamic, forward movement with which we have been endowed, so that we can constantly continue to journey toward God. No matter how much progress we may make, our journey will never be ended this side of eternity. God wants us to keep searching, finding, and enjoying, that we may truly be filled to capacity, and that our very capacity for God may constantly increase.

But how do we come to know this God whom our restless nature seeks to possess? What is our God like? In his *Confessions* Augustine points out some of the characteristics which make God so appealing. The entire passage is well worth reading and reflecting, but here is a sampling:

> You are most hidden and yet most present to us at the same time, most beautiful and most strong, firmly established and yet we cannot comprehend you . . . You love us in a kindly way, desire us, but without apprehension; you are troubled because of our faults, but you suffer no pain . . . You restore all you find, though you never lost them. You have no needs, but you rejoice in what you gain. You are always generous, yet you do demand interest on your gifts . . . You forgive us

our debts, but suffer no loss as a result . . . Yet who can really say anything about you? [Conf 1, 4].

In this passage Augustine is really giving his readers some powerful reasons for knowing, searching for, and finding God. For though God has nothing to gain from us, we have everything to gain from God. God gives us many gifts and, like the landowner in the gospel who entrusted his possessions to others while he was absent, God wants to see these gifts utilized, multiplied, expanded, and shared with others.

As we have seen from our brief consideration of the prophet Jeremiah, God knows us intimately and invites us to respond to his call so that we might come to know him better. To make this easier God reveals himself to us in many different ways: *through nature*–St. Paul's Letter to the Romans speaks loud and clear about this; *through the Scriptures,* which is God's spoken Word; *through the sacraments* of the Church, and most of all the Eucharist. But in a very special way God has revealed himself *through his Son Jesus Christ.* "Philip, after I have been with you all this time, you still do not know me? Whoever has seen me has seen the Father . . . Do you not believe that I am in the Father and the Father is in me?" [John 14:9-10]. How could one be more precise than that?

Jesus teaches us by his life and message what our God and Father is really like. God is compassion, God is understanding, God is justice, God is mercy. Above all, God is love. And how we do need to experience these traits firsthand in our own lives! Moreover, if we truly believe that we are all made in the image and likeness of our God, then we will understand that God can and does also speak to us through other men and women, maybe even when we least expect it, as happened to Augustine. Augustine did not realize it at the time, but many people who crossed his path in life were living and free instruments of God's very real presence to him. He only came to realize this later, as he looked back on what had happened to him. I am sure all of us can relate to that fact. Often it is only in hindsight that we realize how much love God really has shown us in using those close to us, as well as those who may be very much against us, to wake us from our slumber and direct us more clearly back to the right path, or even on to greater and higher goals.

We are also called to know God by prayer, and not just by a prayer made up of words. God knows how to communicate with us very well when we simply allow ourselves time for silence, time away from the constant noise of everyday life. But more about this in another chapter.

Augustine longed for true happiness, but as he tells us, he was afraid to look for it in God. Yes, he truly suspected it existed in God, but he was afraid of what this might cost him, afraid that he would have to give up his search for wealth, prestige, and sexual pleasure, those very goals which he had set as his highest priorities before baptism [see Conf 6, 6]. As a youth he had prayed for the gift of chastity, but he was not really serious about it, so his prayer became one that showed his fear, his weakness, and his lack of trust in God and himself:

> In my youth . . . I had prayed to you for chastity, saying: "Give me chastity and continence, but not yet!" I was really afraid that you would quickly answer my prayer and cure me all too soon of the disease of lust, which I preferred to have satisfied rather than snuffed out [Conf 8, 7].

Only later in life was Augustine able to realize that God alone can satisfy us.

To seek to know ourselves and to know God better is to open ourselves to a marvelous adventure, the adventure of a lifetime, and though it may lead to some frustration, it can also bring us to grow and to know true peace in our hearts. Happiness—true happiness—is not the result of just knowing things or even knowing about God, but rather of appreciating life and the mystery of God's love—and then doing something about it. It is just as Augustine says: "A person of faith owns the entire wealth of the world, for even though he has almost nothing as his own, if he clings to you, Lord, whom all things serve, he has everything" [Conf 5, 4]. It should be a real joy for all of us to help others understand the mystery of themselves, their call to greatness as sons and daughters of God, and God's tremendous love for them. Augustine encourages all of us to keep moving forward constantly, because growth involves movement, and movement means there is life.

> It should not be necessary for me to always have to tell you things as though they were new. It is true, however, that we ourselves must be new people, and not let what is old get in our way. We must grow and make progress . . . We do not make progress by returning to our former condition in life, but by growing in the newness that is ours [On Ps 131, 1].

3

What Does It Mean To Be a Christian Today?

The story is told of a very wise old Russian Holy Man, who had lived alone for most of his life deep in the forest near a small village. Word spread that he was about to leave the area, so the prior of a nearby monastery of Russian monks went to see him to bid him farewell. The Holy Man and the prior prayed and chatted together for several hours. Then when it was time for the prior to leave, he asked the Holy Man: When is the Messiah going to return? How will we recognize him? The wise old man smiled, embraced the prior, and whispered in his ear: *The Messiah has already returned; he is in your monastery.*

All the way home through the woods, for the next hour and a half, the prior reflected on those farewell words of the Holy Man. How can this be? he asked himself. There are only five of us. I know I am not the Messiah. Certainly it could not be Brother John; he is not at all learned. But how about Stephen? Maybe it is Stephen. He is so quiet and thoughtful. Then again there is Isaac, who works so hard, but is also so hard to get along with. Could he be the Messiah? And of course there is also our doorkeeper, Felix. He is always praying. Could he be the one?

When the prior arrived home, he shared with the other four how his visit had gone. And he told them about the Holy Man's final message: The Messiah is among you. None of them could believe it, but then each one went off and began reflecting on that statement. What if . . . ?, they asked themselves. But they were always stymied by one another's weaknesses: one had no learning, the other was too quiet, the third worked hard but was a real pain to live with, and one prayed all day but did nothing else. Of course they thought about the prior also, even though he denied being the Messiah. Slowly, however, they all noticed that they were thinking more positively about one another, that there was greater harmony than before in their little community, that each one began esteeming the others more highly, and that each one began seeking to serve the others, rather than to be served. Then they realized the wisdom of the old Holy Man. By placing the identity of the Messiah in such nebulous terms, he had made them do some real soul-searching. The result: they experienced a greater desire to seek God and to find God in others, despite their weaknesses. Love for one another grew more rapidly than it had in many years.

That's the essence of the story as I remember it, and it is a truly fascinating tale. For me it seems to sum up the message that Jesus left us: if you would really be my disciples, then you must love one another as I have loved you. This is the way all peoples will recognize you as my followers: that you love one another [see John 13:35].

These thoughts of Jesus are two thousand years old, but they still pack a wallop, they are still very powerful and very meaningful, and they are still the answer to so many of the problems that our world suffers from. Some people have said that Christianity has had its day and it has not worked; just look at the mess we are in today. Those who are more honest and objective will respond that Christianity has been around for two thousand years, but it has rarely been practiced or lived as Jesus taught it; many people have not given it a fair chance, not even many who call themselves Christians.

Who Is a Christian?

Which brings us to a more important question: What or who is a Christian? And specifically: What does it mean for you to be a Christian?

For me being a Christian is to have received a call to a new life, a life with God which involves a radical change from within, which involves a shift from the priorities which the world usually sets before us to priorities that Jesus has given us in the name of his Father. We live in the "ME" generation, a time when the individual is so exalted that everyone and everything else seems to take second place. That is not what Jesus taught. Jesus put God first, and asked us to love our neighbor in the same way we love ourselves. Augustine too is very clear in his approach to the love we owe one another: "You say that you love Christ? Keep his commandment and love your brother and sister. But if you do not love them, how can you be said to love him whose commandment you actually despise?" [On 1 John 9, 11].

Augustine also insists that, "It would be hard to find anyone who does not have some way to do good for others" [S 91, 9]. And he gives examples galore: those with funds can give to the poor, help the needy, build churches if they wish. Others with fewer material possessions can give good advice, be an example of holiness, share learning, recall those who stray, seek out the lost. Even the very poor can share what they have, not so much in a material way, but by being available to those who have even fewer possibilities than they themselves, and by giving a clear example of love and selflessness [see S 91, 1].

The Joy of Being a Christian

To be a Christian—to carry out this chief commandment of Jesus Christ—was the source of the greatest joy Augustine could imagine. He set being a Christian in contrast with his call to be a bishop and pointed out in a striking manner what the Christian call meant to him:

> Though I am terrified by what I am for you, I am comforted by what I am with you. For you I am a bishop, but with you I am a Christian. The first is the name of an office I have accepted, the second is a grace. The first involves danger, the second salvation. If the fact that I have been redeemed with you makes me happier than being set over you, then, as our Lord commands, I shall be more tirelessly your servant. Other-

wise I would fear being ungrateful for the redemption which has made me worthy to be your fellow servant [S 340, 1].

For Augustine, Christianity was the way to salvation and redemption from sin. It was a grace, a gift shared with all other Christians, a condition that brought consolation and that at the same time allowed him and other followers of Christ to be fellow-servants of one another. And he further reminded his people: "We are not Christians except on account of a future life. People should neither hope for blessings in this life, nor promise themselves the happiness of this world because they are Christians" [On Ps 92, 1].

Such a statement reminds me very much of St. Paul's admonition: "If Christ has not been raised [from the dead], our preaching is void of content and your faith is empty too . . . [it] is worthless" [1 Cor 15:14-16]. Jesus overcame sin and death. The promise has been extended to us Christians also, that with God's grace we can do likewise: we too can overcome sin and death. This is beautifully expressed in the Preface of the Mass for the Dead, where we hear, "Life is changed, not taken away." We shall indeed die, but it is not all over by any means. We shall rise as Jesus did. Therefore, we are called to be a people of great hope!

Augustine has strong words for those who pretend to be what they are not, who have a title or a job and do not live up to it. He never hesitated to call to task even some of his fellow bishops who put their own honor before the health of their people: "He is called a bishop, but that he is not. For him the title is an empty one" [S 340A, 4].

> To have a title and not live up to it, to enjoy a name and not the reality, is of no use to anyone. There are many called physicians who cannot cure; there are many called night watchmen, but they sleep all night. There are also many called Christians, but in fact they are not Christians at all, because what they are supposed to be they do not show in their life, manners, faith, hope, or love" [On 1 John 4, 4].

The power of the name of Jesus made itself felt in Augustine's life from his mother's breast, as an infant. She taught him to revere that name, and it stuck with him even during those fifteen years of his wandering among various sects and philosophies. Perhaps it was this very fact, that he had been among the straying sheep for so long, that prompted him to teach his people not to judge others or count them as lost just because they were not Christians, or even if they were worshipers of sticks and stones. In other words, we cannot read the future; we cannot know how God's grace will act on people.

> Even before someone becomes a Christian, you do not know what he or she looks like in God's sight, or what God has foreknown about that person. Sometimes the one you laugh at for worshiping sticks and stones is converted and worships the true God, more religiously perhaps than you. There are many close neighbors of ours hidden away among those who are not in the Church; and there are many hiding in the Church who are in fact miles away from us. And since we cannot read the future, we should treat everyone as our neighbor, not only because we share the common lot of mortals on this earth, but also because we hope for that inheritance in heaven, and we do not know who is going to share it with us [On Ps 25: S 2, 2].

We must never give up on others, anymore than Monica ever gave up on Augustine as he wandered spiritually. She prayed, she wept, she sought counsel, she reached out to others, she lived her faith to the hilt. On the whole she took a gentle approach to winning Augustine back to the faith, one which in the end succeeded. What an example of a Christian mother Monica is even today!

Augustine proposes the same approach to bringing others to Christ, urging his people to win others for Christ, yes, but gently, kindly [see On Ps 33: S 2, 6–7]. As St. Francis de Sales put it in one of his writings: "More flies will be attracted to a teaspoonful of honey than to a barrel of vinegar." Kindness and gentleness have a way of winning over even the most adamant of people. Attacking them will rarely if ever do anything to help them find Christ.

A few years back I was sent to a fine parish in the Midwest to preach for our Augustinian missionaries in Peru.

While there, I was informed of another missionary who had been there sometime before me, trying to stir the people of that parish to give generously to his third world mission in Africa. But he made a terrible mistake. He literally attacked the people as being too well off; he told them they owed their money to the missions. Needless to say, many parishioners were turned off by his negative approach. He did not touch their hearts, as he easily could have. He failed to be gentle and kind, as he could have been. It was his mission that suffered the consequences of a meager collection.

Qualities of the Christian Life

What are some of the qualities you look for in a Christian, qualities that make these people like magnets who draw others to ask why they are as they are? Often we are not even aware of some of our own qualities that may be attractive to others. Before you continue here, let me ask you to write down or make a mental note of some of the qualities you like to find in Christians. This will come in handy further on in this chapter.

I will give you an example of a couple I know who radiate fine Christian qualities. He is a middle-aged layman whom I have known for several years now. After his ordination as a permanent deacon, he was continually astounded at the way people sought counsel from both himself and his wife, who had accompanied him in his course preparation for the deaconate. This couple leads a very simple life, but they share a generous and gentle enthusiasm for the faith. They are prayerful both as individuals and as a couple, and they are totally dedicated to the Church and to helping others who are interested in learning about the Catholic faith. While they clearly recognize their own weaknesses, they gladly share with others the gifts God has given them. It is certainly Christians like these that make the faith attractive to those outside the Church, as well as to those who profess the same beliefs.

While I am sure you have already come up with your own list of prized Christian qualities, I would like to offer you a list of my own, though these qualities are certainly not exclusive. Selfless love, of course, is basic to anyone who claims the name Christian. But beyond this basic virtue, these are some of the characteristics I would like to find in a Christian—and of course in myself: *happiness, courage, enthusiasm, and humility.*

1. HAPPINESS. How could we not be happy if we recognize that God is our friend? That the Spirit of God dwells within us? That we have been given the grace to resist sin and overcome temptation? I am not speaking about a bubbly, superficial kind of happiness, but a happiness that is rooted in the heart, that can be present even in the midst of suffering and pain. "You are my friends," says Jesus, "if you do what I command you" [John 15:14]. Jesus' commands are not impossible, even though they are demanding: basically we are asked to love one another, as Jesus has loved us. That may sound easy, yet it creates conflict in many people, especially when we are told that we should even love our enemies in the same way. That is so difficult, and yet forgiving others frees us from a terrible burden that can consume our hearts and make us most unhappy. Jesus knew what he was talking about. Love is liberating; true love makes for true happiness.

2. COURAGE. Do I have the courage of my convictions? Am I willing to stand up for what I believe in the face of peer pressure or other kinds of pressure, in the atmosphere of our present secular society with its materialistic and frequently hedonistic values? As a child I used to read about the many martyrs of the early Church. I had no idea that martyrdom was something Christians would still have to face in my times. But history was repeating itself even as I grew up. One of my first recollections as a nine-year-old was a headline in our local newspaper, which read something like this: "100 Augustinians from the Escorial Killed in Spain." That headline of course referred to what happened at the beginning of the Spanish Civil War [1936–1939], when government troops started persecuting priests and religious. Since then, how many others have laid down their lives for Christ in all parts of the world: Mexico, Nicaragua, the Congo, China! But most of us are not asked to make that supreme sacrifice. Our Christian courage must rather show itself in the market-

place, at home, in our places of work, in our social relationships. What kind of an example for their own lives do other people find in us?

This question reminds me of a sermon Augustine once gave to his newly baptized adults on Easter Sunday. They were just about to lay aside the symbolic white garments which they had worn since their baptism during the Easter Vigil and return to the hum-drum and the temptations of their daily existence. But as Augustine sent them back to their family life, their social contacts, and their work, he had these sound words of advice for them, which we can easily take to heart ourselves:

> Choose for yourselves whom you will imitate: those who fear God, those who enter the house of God with reverence, who attentively listen to the word of God, keep it in mind, meditate on it, and carry it out. These are the ones you should choose to imitate . . . Begin to live well and you will see how many others gather round you and what a great fraternity you enjoy. [And then with great realism Augustine added this thought, which is exactly what we all need to hear:] But suppose you cannot find anyone to imitate? What then? Well then, be yourself such that others can imitate you! [S 228, 2].

3. ENTHUSIASM. Enthusiasm, like happiness, is an interior quality. It is a gift of the Spirit and can be given by no one but the Spirit. It is not the quickly lost enthusiasm associated with athletic contests. Nor is it the kind of enthusiasm that is longer-lasting, but associated with a special project, adventure, or trip, for example. Rather, the enthusiasm I speak of is the kind that is constantly alive within our hearts, like burning coals, providing energy for the many routine affairs of life and ready to burst into flame for those more important moments and challenges which come to each of us, frequently at the most unexpected times. This is the kind of enthusiasm that Augustine describes as true love: "O fiery Love, which is never extinguished! O Charity, my God, set me on fire with that same love!" [Conf 10, 29].

4. HUMILITY. It would be hard for me to imagine a happy, enthusiastic, and courageous Christian who was not at the

same time humble about self and the call to follow Christ. Christians practice humility not only when they do not brag about what they accomplish but more importantly when they recognize that without the life of Jesus that flows through them they would be helpless to do anything really good. Humble people recognize their humanity, the fact that we are all humans and therefore weak, the fact that, as Jesus said: "The one who lives in me and I in him will produce abundant fruit, for without me you can do nothing" [John 15:5]. Humble people are open to the working of God in their lives; God is welcome in their hearts. That is not the case with the proud. They believe they already have everything they need; God cannot even get close to them. God is effectively shut out of their lives because they simply do not feel the need for him!

> God looks at us from within; that is where he examines and weighs us . . . You can see that the reason why God hears prayers is because the person says to God: "I am afflicted and poor." Be sure that you are indeed afflicted and poor; otherwise you will not be heard. If you find any basis within you or around you for being presumptuous, rid yourself of it; let your whole trust be in God. Be in need of him, and he will fill you [On Ps 86, 3].

There is an age-old question that has always challenged me since I first heard it. It is a question that goes to the very heart of things, no matter what qualities we may propose as those that should mark a genuine Christian life. The question is simply this: *If you were accused of being a Christian in a court of law, would there be enough evidence to convict you?* If the judge and jury were really impartial and interested only in doing what was right, would they be able to find enough evidence from your life, from the testimony of those who know and love you, and even from those who may hate you, to build a good case, to be able to say without fear of mistake: that person is truly a Christian? This question takes us right back to that earlier quote from Augustine, about those who claim to be what they are not [see above, p. 29, On 1 John 4, 4].

A Key Word: Influence

The qualities I have just mentioned are those I would like to find in any Christian. But I believe there is another key factor which every Christian must take cognizance of, and especially those who are in any position of responsibility. That factor is this: every Christian is called to be a leader, and, like it or not, a leader will always influence others. A leader is not necessarily one who commands or is in charge of others, but a leader is *always* one who by actions, ideas, and ideals is influential in the lives of others, either for good or for evil. And what is most interesting in all this is the fact that sometimes the person being influenced is not at all aware of how much he or she is being affected, just as the leader can also be totally unaware of the influence he or she is exerting on others.

An example that comes immediately to my mind concerns Augustine's relationship with St. Ambrose. Augustine was drawn to Ambrose, the bishop of Milan, not because he was preaching about Jesus and his message, but because Ambrose was such a polished speaker. Slowly but surely, however, without Augustine even being aware of it, the content of Ambrose's message began to get through to Augustine's heart and mind, along with the satisfaction he experienced in listening to Ambrose's style. Could Ambrose have been aware of the impact he was having then and there on this proud, young philosopher? I seriously doubt it. But later on Augustine certainly saw God's hand in all this, as he remarks in his *Confessions:* "Without my being aware of it, Lord, I was led to Ambrose by you, so that with full awareness I might be led by him to you" [Conf 5, 13].

That kind of influence was positive. But consider this other scenario. We are all aware of the tremendous influence that young leaders or youth groups exert on their peers. This can be a good thing, such as when you bring youths together for positive purposes in school or parish settings. But in other situations peers who are leaders can bring enormous pressure to bear on other young individuals to "conform" in thought, word, dress, and action, even to the extent of doing things that are very contrary to what they have been taught and know is right. That is pure peer pressure, and it can be devastating. All of us have been influenced by many different people in our lives up to now. Before we finish our pilgrimage through life, many others will affect us, will bring to bear their influence on us, whether they know it or not. In the same way, we too have influenced many people already, and many others will yet be affected by us—for good or for ill—as we continue our journey through life. Most likely we have not always been aware of our influence on others, nor will we necessarily be aware of it even in the future.

As Augustine looked back on his life, he constantly saw the hand of God in the people who influenced him throughout his journey, and especially when he was searching for the truth and wandering far away from the Catholic faith. What he experienced may well remind us of how we ourselves have been influenced by others, or how we may have influenced and affected them. Augustine was influenced by family and friends, by teachers and peers, by strangers and even enemies. He was influenced in favorable and unfavorable ways. What made him most grateful was the fact that God had chosen to work through so many different people to bring him to his senses.

The Greatest Example: Jesus Christ

But if we are looking for examples of influence and leadership, we must not neglect to speak about that one who is the greatest example for all of us, Jesus Christ. Jesus was a born leader, and as such he influenced others on a broad scale, inviting some explicitly to follow him, while encouraging others in their way of life by his word and example. We know that his close disciples were invited in a very special way to turn aside from what they had been doing in order to follow him. Some had been fishermen, others tax collectors, or engaged in other activities. But they left everything to follow in his footsteps. By doing so they may have thought they were giving up much, but they acquired much more than they ever could have had in their former walks of life. At the same time they witnessed events that were startling (such as some of Jesus' miracles), and they built up their confidence in him, only to find it all seemingly crushed when Jesus suffered his passion and death.

Unfortunately, there was one among the disciples who did not have that confidence in Jesus that the others had. Judas refused to let the Master's good influence turn him away from his bad habits and his self-seeking. He even contributed directly to Jesus' death. Judas was a perfect example of the fact that leadership of even the finest kind, of the kind that Jesus put into play, is helpless unless people are open to improvement.

Hope was restored for the other apostles, however, in an entirely new and unexpected way when Jesus appeared to them, risen from the dead. The disciples had been totally distraught by the Master's rejection and death. They had failed to understand what his mission really was, even though he had sought to teach them about it. They had put their trust in him in a merely human way, looking for human results and glory that were not to be forthcoming. With the resurrection, however, they began to see life from a different point of view. Through Jesus and the Spirit which he sent upon them, they found new strength, an increase in faith, and a new meaning to life.

The interesting part about all this is that, after the coming of the Spirit, the apostles immediately began to exercise leadership themselves, though formerly they certainly did not seem to have been aware that they possessed this quality. The influence they began to have on others did not come merely or even principally from their charismatic selves—if that they were!—but *from the power of God working through them*. Where courage had formerly been lacking, it was now present in abundance. Whereas beforehand they had been very concerned about what they were going to receive from following Christ, now they were more interested in what the community would receive from their preaching and efforts. Whereas formerly they had been moved by self-interest, now they were moved by an outgoing love. They began to realize a little better their human weaknesses and the power of God making up for their failings in many ways. Because they loved, they were willing to risk, to put themselves on the line for Jesus and his message. Theirs was a real transformation brought about by the initiative of God and their own cooperation.

Augustine, too, just like the Apostles, realized the need to put his whole trust in God because he well understood his great weaknesses. Just as St. Paul would state that he could do all things through God who gave him strength [1 Cor 1:31], so Augustine would pray: "Strengthen me, Lord, that I may have your strength. Give me the grace to do what you command, and command me to do whatever you will!" [Conf 10, 31].

What did the disciples show as they began to be conspicuous leaders in the Church? They reflected courage, community spirit, outgoing love, recognition of the power of God, a willingness to risk. But at the same time, they were still themselves, with all their weaknesses. They failed at times, they made mistakes, some of them serious. But they did not let these mistakes keep them down. If our mistakes teach us something, if we can draw profit from them, no matter how miserable they may make us feel, then they have not been totally negative experiences.

Let me give you a personal example. A few years ago I buried a very dear friend, an Augustinian a few years older than I, who had worked with me in Rome for many years in a position of great responsibility. From my position of leadership, I had put him in charge of the Augustinian Order's secretariat for justice and peace, and he was totally dedicated to what he was trying to do in that position. But on one occasion he confronted me with a very terse question: "Are you really interested in spreading this justice and peace movement in the Order? If you are, you sure don't show it." Needless to say, his blunt honesty was a real wake-up call. I had to reconsider what I was doing, or better, what I was not doing in this regard. My friend had touched a delicate chord and made me reflect deeply on what was going on. This completely changed my approach to this situation.

God shows his loving care for us through ever so many people he sends into our lives, or through those whom we simply happen to meet briefly on our journey through life. The other side of this marvelous truth is that we too are called to have a share in this work, to be willing instruments of God's loving care toward others, often without even knowing that we are influencing others or even how we may be doing it. What is important is that we be open to allowing God to use us for such purposes when and as he pleases. When we have that disposition, God is very likely to take full advantage of our good will, and in ways we cannot even imagine. It is both humbling and consoling to have people tell you, maybe years after the fact, just what an influence something you said or did has had on them. God never ceases to work in mysterious ways. What is truly wonderful is that we ourselves—all of us—are called to be a part of those mysterious ways.

A Joyful Struggle

The Christian life is *a struggle,* but a joyful struggle to overcome the power of evil and to bring greater happiness to others, as well as to ourselves. There will be times in the lives of all of us when we fail to be what we claim to be as Christians. But then that is why Jesus also left us the sacrament of reconciliation, why he gave the gift of forgiveness to his apostles, to pass along to others. Augustine reminds his people of this struggle and of the difficulty of being what they are in this passage:

> If you hope in the Lord . . . don't hide your hope in your heart as though it were a crime. As a matter of fact, scarcely anyone has objection taken to him as a Christian in our times . . . And yet, my brothers and sisters, just you start actually living like a Christian, any of you listening to me now, and see if people don't object, even people who claim to be Christians, though they are certainly not Christian in the way they live. You simply would not believe it unless you had experienced it [On Ps 30:S 3, 7].

My experience parallels that of Augustine: it is often fellow Christians who create the greatest number of difficulties for those who genuinely set themselves to live the Christian life. Why? Perhaps it is because they feel threatened. They do not want their own shortcomings and weaknesses to be shown up, which easily happens when others try to live the gospel message in its fullness, without being selective.

It is quite easy to wear a gold or silver cross around one's neck as a pendant. I know many people who do this. But this is not what makes them or us Christians, any more than a Roman collar or a cassock makes a man a priest. That cross and that collar are external signs, which ought to indicate something about those who wear them. But unless the words and actions of these persons correspond with those external signs, they are meaningless—or better said, they are even false indicators, sometimes to the extent of being hypocritical.

Is it possible to lead a good Christian life today? Yes, but not by ourselves, not alone. We need one another. We need the strength of the Christian community. Above all, we need the strength and courage that comes from prayer and the indwelling of the Holy Spirit. By ourselves we will not be able to overcome the many obstacles that we experience all around us. With God, however, all things are possible. As Jesus reminds us: "Take courage! I have overcome the world" [John 16:33].

Jesus never denied that it would be difficult to follow him along the way that leads to God. But he guaranteed the way would be there for those wishing to walk it; he himself would be that way. And he gave his first disciples clearly encouraging words to reflect on as he prepared to leave them, words which we too can reflect on very fruitfully as we take to heart this message of truly being Christians for our times.

> I am the vine, you are the branches. He who lives in me and I in him will produce abundantly, for apart from me you can do nothing . . . As the Father has loved me, so I have loved you. Live on in my love. You will live in my love if you keep my commandments . . . All this I tell you that my joy may be yours and your joy may be complete [John 15:5, 9-11].

4

Struggling to Find God:
Augustine's Odyssey and Ours

I teach Augustine's *Confessions* to high school students. That might seem like a daunting task, and it is—until we make some headway into this classic. In the beginning the students cannot really understand why this book might still be so widely read sixteen hundred years after it was written. Then all of a sudden it hits them: Augustine's story is their story, our story! His attractions, concerns, temptations, falls, sins, and eventual rise to a new life are still part of Christian living even today.

Let me offer two examples from Augustine's youth. When he was fifteen, during a year of idleness from his studies, Augustine was drawn into a group of peers who vandalized a neighbor's orchard, where there were many pear trees. He did not need the pears, nor did the other boys. But he did need their companionship; peer pressure was no different then than now. He also loved the sin itself, that is, asserting his independence from God's law and doing what he wanted. In fact, like many others who sin, without realizing it he wanted to be his own lawmaker, to decide for himself what was right or wrong, without any reference to reality or God's revelation.

In his puberty he was overwhelmed by lust. A hot temperament merely added fuel to the fire. He thought his mother's counsel about avoiding sex outside of marriage to be pure "womanish" advice. Nothing new there! Until much later in life he failed to see that God, whom he blamed for being too silent in his regard, had been trying to get through to him all the time by means of that loving mother and her all too "womanish" advice. Augustine just had not been listening.

It is no wonder, then, that even today's youth can understand how Augustine's adolescence and young manhood present them with some of the identical challenges that they must face. It is no wonder that adults to whom I have taught this same course on the *Confessions* are also stunned by the reality of it all, as they reflect back on their own youth, or realize how it is being lived out again in their adolescent children.

Augustine did not grow up without faith. His mother taught him from his tenderest years to love and honor the name of Jesus [Conf 3, 4; 6, 4]. As a child he had pleaded for baptism during a severe illness, but when he suddenly recovered his health this was denied him. Apparently infant baptism was not practiced in North Africa in the middle of the fourth century. But he was a catechumen, a learner in the faith, as he tells us, and he always considered himself to be such, even though he appeared to give up his beginner's Christianity when he joined a sect called the Manichees.

Drifting Away

But as the purpose of this chapter is to look more closely at Augustine's search for the truth, and consequently for God, I think we should principally listen to what Augustine himself tells us about this, as he describes the very human obstacles he met up with along this difficult and painful journey. I believe the description of his own search and struggle will help us understand much better what frequently happens when people search for the truth and for God.

What were some of the elements in his journey away from and finally back to the faith? There were rising passions, pride, and theological errors; a fruitless search for purely human wisdom; slow disillusionment with the wholly unsatisfactory explanations of those who claimed to have all the answers and did not; wavering and uncertainty in a type of spiritual "limbo"; the stimulating grace of both St. Ambrose's preaching and the stories told him by some people he admired; and a growing discontent with himself. All of these and many other elements contributed to his finally reaching the saving grace of his conversion.

Passion and Pride

Augustine's wanderings were, in the beginning, essentially no different from those of ever so many teenagers and young people from the beginning of time to our own day. As he himself tells us, in his sixteenth year, a year of idleness at home because of lack of money for studies, "the brambles of passion overwhelmed my mind and there was no one to weed them out" [Conf 2, 3]. He blames his parents for not having been more attentive to his needs, though the solution of marriage which he proposed was hardly what would have been most helpful for a fifteen year old. He boasted to his peers about bad things he had never done so that he might not be considered "different." He implied in the following text that he was indeed trying to live a more chaste life than some others he associated with, but he did not want them to know this!

> I was so blind as to be ashamed of not being as shameless as my companions . . . If I had not done enough evil to make myself equal to the truly wicked, I would make up things that I had not really done. For I feared appearing more contemptible because more innocent, or more wicked because I was more chaste [Conf 2, 3].

What Augustine speaks of here is a mirror of what probably most young people go through during the time of puberty, as they seek to curry the favor and admiration of their friends and peers. When he was sixteen or seventeen he went to study at the finest school in North Africa, the University of Carthage (in modern-day Tunisia), and quite quickly his separation from the faith of his home life began to be even more pronounced:

I wanted to love and I was searching for something to love. I spurned security or a path free of pitfalls. I was famished for that interior food, which is yourself, my God, but I was not aware of this need. I had no desire for the food that does not perish, not because I had been filled by it, but because the more I was deprived of it, the less desirable it seemed [Conf 3, 1].

When he was eighteen, Cicero's *Hortensius* fell into his hands. This book of the famous Roman statesman, who lived before Christ, was used by God as an external grace to shake Augustine up, to fill him with a great desire for wisdom. As Augustine put it:

That book changed my view of things. It changed the very way I prayed to you, Lord, and it stirred up within me new hopes and aspirations. All at once it made my empty desires seem repulsive, and it made me long for the wisdom of eternal truth with an unbelievable and heartfelt desire. I began to rise up so that I could find my way back to you [Conf 3, 4].

He began to find his way out of the depths to which he had sunk. But as he tells us, he was not successful. Why not? Augustine tells us he could not find the name of Christ in that book, and though this disappointed him greatly, it also encouraged him to examine the Christian Scriptures. But here his pride intervened and kept him from getting beyond a superficial reading of these sacred books. Accustomed as he was to reading the classical Latin authors, he balked at the language of the Scriptures, which he found totally unworthy of comparison with the nobility of Cicero's writings: "My swollen pride detested their simplicity, and my sharp mind was unable to get to the bottom of their profound thought" [Conf 3, 5]. He could not understand their content because he was completely taken up by externals, such as grammar and structure.

Still in search of light and wisdom, but blinded by pride, he fell in with the Manichees, a sect which proposed a mixture of Zoroastrianism and Christianity, and which promised to solve all his problems through the pure light of reason. With this his error grew. He was trapped, but he did not realize it. "Nearly nine years passed during which I wallowed deep in the mire and the darkness of error. I tried to get up many times, but every time I was hurled back down all the more painfully" [Conf 3, 11].

God's "Holy Bait": St. Ambrose

Those nine years of which Augustine speaks had ultimately taken him far from his homeland of North Africa: first from Carthage to Rome, and then to Milan, on the way to honor and fame among some of the more powerful people of the times. But none of this filled him with any lasting happiness. In his *Confessions* he gives expression to the deep hopelessness that he experienced at that time:

> I was walking in the darkness and on a slippery path. I was looking for you outside myself, and I could not find you because you are the God of my heart. I had reached the bottom of the ocean, had lost all faith and was without hope of finding the truth [Conf 6, 1].

Precisely because of this sense of helplessness, Augustine was becoming ripe for further special graces. On his own admission—a most important element!—he had scratched bottom, so to speak. His pride was cracking, because it was failing to bring him the true happiness he had been seeking. He no longer trusted either himself or the Manichees. As a matter of fact, he had begun to abandon these Manichees a few years earlier, because they were incapable of answering his sharp questions about their teachings with any degree of satisfaction. The grace that was given him at this stage of his journey was both very special and very subtle also: he came to know Ambrose, the saintly bishop of Milan, who was also a great preacher. His style and delivery enthralled Augustine and became the "holy bait" which God used to draw Augustine to see the Scriptures from an entirely different point of view. "I did not bother to learn what Ambrose was saying. I was only listening to the style of his preaching . . . Still the very essence of what he was saying, which I tried to ignore, was reaching my heart together with his words, which I loved to hear" [Conf 5, 14]:

Every Sunday I listened to him as he very correctly explained the word of truth to the people. It became ever more clear to me that all the difficulties which had been woven against the Sacred Scriptures by those who had deceived me with their cunning lies could be dispelled . . . I blushed joyfully that for so many years I had been howling my complaints not against the Catholic faith but against some figment of my own imagination. I had been rash and irreverent because I had spoken out in condemnation of those things about which I had not taken the trouble to be better informed [Conf 6, 3].

But despite the fact that some light from the Scriptures was finally getting through to his heart, he found himself stymied again, because he was seeking mathematical certainty in the realm of the spiritual: "I would not let my heart consent in any way, because I was afraid of a sheer fall, but the suspense was killing me even more surely . . . Then, O Lord, little by little you touched my heart in a most gentle and merciful way and gave me understanding . . ." [Conf 6, 4–5].

Final Waverings

But Augustine was still procrastinating, afraid to leave behind what he knew did not satisfy him and embrace what he did not yet know sufficiently:

I was greatly astonished when I finally brought myself to reflect on the long time that had passed from my nineteenth year, when I had first begun to burn with desire for the knowledge of wisdom . . . And here I was already thirty years old and still vacillating in the same quagmire because of my greed to enjoy the present passing and fading things. And all the time I was saying, "Tomorrow I shall discover the truth. It will be very clear to me and I shall make it my own. Faustus will come and explain everything" [Conf 6, 11].

Faustus was the chief Manichean bishop, who was supposed to be able to answer all his questions. As a matter of fact, when Faustus did come and could not answer Augustine's difficulties, Augustine realized that the Manicheans did not have what he was looking for. It freed him in an extraordinary way to look further and elsewhere for the truth.

But Augustine was also still bound tightly by the power of his passions: "Though I longed for a happy life, I was afraid to find it where it actually was. And so I sought it by running away from it. I thought I would be too miserable without a woman's love" [Conf 6, 11].

The two years that were yet to pass till his conversion were years marked by great interior struggle and torment: "You knew what I endured [Lord] but no human being knew it" [Conf 7, 7]. Though he was still a victim of pride and passion, there were also quiet moments during these months, moments of light and grace that encouraged him:

> I was amazed that I now loved you and not some phantom in your place. But I was not secure in the enjoyment of my God. I was drawn to you by your beauty, but I was quickly drawn away from you by my own weight, which kept dragging me back to the things of the earth. This weight was the power of the flesh. But I carried your remembrance with me, and I had no doubt at all that you were the one to whom I should cling . . . [Conf 7, 17].

Simplicianus, the elderly priest who had converted Ambrose and baptized him, was the next of God's unusual graces in Augustine's life. After Augustine had poured out his heart to this holy man, Simplicianus instructed him about the conversion of the great Roman professor of rhetoric, Victorinus, who twenty years earlier had willingly given up his teaching career for his new-found faith in Christ. (Christians had been forbidden to teach literature and speech by a law of Emperor Julian at this time: see Conf 8, 5.) All of which made Augustine reflect on how happy Victorinus had been, and how unhappy he himself still was to be bound by his long-unresisted habit.

The Grace of Conversion

God's final mercy to Augustine was triggered by the visit of a countryman from North Africa, who then held high office at the court of the emperor in Milan, a certain Ponticianus. Augustine was staying with Alypius, his very close friend, when the visitor arrived. Ponticianus spoke to the two of them about the monks of Egypt and Milan, as well as about the recent conversion to the monastic life of two important state officials. What happened in Augustine's heart then and what followed can only be properly told, once again, in Augustine's own words, for the long-awaited moment of grace was finally at hand: "While Ponticianus was speaking, Lord, you made me turn back to look at myself. You took me from behind my back where I had hid so that I would not have to look at myself . . . And so I saw myself and I was horrified, and there was now no place to hide" [Conf 8, 7].

> My inner self was in turmoil. My heart, my innermost being, was out of control as I turned on Alypius, and exclaimed to him, with looks that betrayed this inner conflict, "What are we doing? What is the meaning of what you have heard?" These uneducated men stand up and storm the gates of heaven while we, for all our senseless learning, lie here groveling in this world of flesh and blood! . . . I said something like this and then my feelings tore me away from him. I left him to gaze at me speechless and astonished [Conf 8, 8].

> When this deep pondering had wretched up all my misery from the depths of my soul and gathered it in the sight of my heart, a huge storm broke loose within me, bringing with it a great flood of tears. So that I might let my heart pour out all these noisy tears, I got up and left Alypius . . . I spoke with you at length, Lord, if not in these very words, at least in this sense: "O Lord, how long? Will you be angry forever? Remember not against us the iniquities of our past." For I felt that I was still held back by my sins, and in my misery I cried out pitifully: "How long shall I go on crying 'tomorrow, tomorrow'? Why not now? Why not make an end of my shameful sins right now?" [Conf 8, 12].

It was at this very point that a strange thing happened. A child's voice, coming from a nearby house, interrupted Augustine's bitter weeping. It was a sing-song voice that chanted over and over again, "Take up and read, Take up and read!" The strange part about all this was that Augustine could not recall any child's game which made use of such a song. He took this, then, as a mysterious call from God to pick up the Scriptures and read the first chapter that should strike his view. At that moment he remembered that Anthony had done something similar when embracing the hermitical life. So he did just that, and what struck his eyes was this passage from Paul's letter to the Romans: "[Not] in carousing and drunkenness, not in sexual excess and lust, not in quarreling and jealousy. Rather, put on the Lord Jesus Christ and make no provision for the desires of the flesh" [Rom 13:13-14].

Augustine comments on the impact this passage had on him in a few brief words that are really the climax of his entire struggle to reach the faith: "I had no desire to read any further, nor was it necessary. For as soon as I finished reading that passage, my heart was flooded with what seemed a light of certainty and all the darkness of doubt was dispelled" [Conf 8, 12].

To carry Augustine's account any further would be anticlimactic. This special grace led not only to his baptism during the Easter Vigil of the following year 387 but also to his renunciation of the attractions of the world and his embracing a consecrated life of service to God upon his return to Africa. And that is sufficient for our purposes at this moment in what concerns Augustine's deep, personal experience with conversion, with finding God.

A Story Like So Many Others

But Augustine's story, in its essential elements, is also the story of ever so many others. Think of those who find Christ for the first time or find their way back to him after a short or prolonged separation. It is also the story of those who, while striving to live close to Christ, find themselves wavering in generosity and in need of renewed dedication. It could also be the story of many others who have fallen into comfortable ruts in life, whose energy has been dulled or sapped by fear of change or renewal (the unknown once again!) or by routine or apathy, and who as a result find it increasingly difficult to break away and entrust themselves to God's Holy Spirit, which would constantly renew us if we allowed it. It is my experience that people who read Augustine's *Confessions* tend to find themselves reflected there in one way or another. That is why I would like to take a few moments to pass in review the key elements in Augustine's journey. This may well help us realize what happens in the depths of many human hearts—maybe even in our own—as these hearts struggle with themselves to grow.

Who is it that could not identify with at least some phase of Augustine's journey toward God, toward the faith: his falls, his sufferings, his wavering, his rising, his turning back to God, his new enthusiasm and generosity? Who has not felt in some way the agony of that interior struggle, that conflict between two parts of our inner selves, with each vying for victory? Who has not experienced his or her own helplessness to make progress alone, without assistance? If there are any among us who have not had some such experience, let them thank God, for they have been blessed with exceptional graces. But there are many—I would say a great majority of men and women—who can feel totally in unison with Augustine in their struggle to reform, to turn back, to renew themselves, or draw closer to Christ and the Father by shaking off even minor obstacles. Does not this also help explain the popularity of the *Confessions* down through the centuries? Bearing all this in mind, let us take another look at those four principal phases of Augustine's journey toward conversion. I think they offer some clear insights into the way many, if not most of us, react from time to time.

First Phase: Running Away from God

Augustine's road to conversion was a long, hard, and at times agonizing, struggle. He suffered all the pitfalls of puberty, and in boasting that he had done bad things which he had not done, he showed himself a victim of human respect and pride, ashamed of innocence and purity rather than vice and sin. He left home to study in another city opening an entirely new world to him that he was eager to take part in, for like almost every growing person, he wanted adventure and freedom. As he put it so succinctly: "I hated security!" How many young people especially must see a part of themselves in all this? The young love adventure and will not let themselves be tied down or limited by that tired old saying: "That is the way we have always done it!"

How many are not exposed to the same dangers as Augustine when they take those first steps away from home, going off to college, for example, to an entirely different environment, where they are away from the guidance of their parents for the first time and very much on their own? And how many for the same reasons—or for others—slowly drift away from God, from the practice of their faith, from what perhaps had been quite appreciated during earlier years at home. This first phase in Augustine's journey is one that is predominantly negative. Moreover, at the same time that it leads away from God, it tends to build up pride to such an extent that people believe they can do anything by themselves alone.

Second Phase: A Search for the Truth, without God

Still, though Augustine had perhaps abandoned God in many ways, God did not abandon Augustine. Cicero's *Hortensius* proved to be a special grace that led Augustine to consult the Scriptures. But his interest was all too brief and his pride too strong. He could not accept this scriptural simplicity, but he did listen to the unsubstantiated promises of the Manichees, who said they could solve all his problems by the light of reason. Among other things, they taught that the world was ruled by two contending principles of good and evil. Augustine was eagerly seeking the truth together with the Manichees, and though his search proved fruitless, at least he was searching; he was not trying to run away from the truth, scary though it can be at times. He struggled with philosophical and theological problems, seeking solutions from the experts of his new-found "faith," only to find himself totally disillusioned by them with the passing of time. For nine or ten years he struggled with fierce intellectual problems before abandoning this sect completely. During this time—the long, second stage of his journey—now and then he tried to get out of what he had come to recognize as a messy situation, but passion and pride kept dragging him back down every time. Is it not much the same today? Passion and pride, in modern dress, keep holding people down through a fierce desire for independence and adventure, a distrust of past solutions for today's woes, an unwarranted confidence in the gurus of science, philosophy, and even spirituality for ready-made solutions—an intense desire to be self-made persons without any outside interference.

Third Phase: Loss of Self-Confidence and Fear of Change

The third phase of Augustine's journey began when he was twenty-eight years old. It was characterized by an admission of defeat, a loss of self-confidence, a feeling of helplessness. Augustine had reached the bottom of the barrel, and he knew it. It was only when he had reached this stage in such a painful fashion that he could really start to profit by the new graces God was already putting before him in the persons of Ambrose, Simplicianus, and Ponticianus. But much as he respected Ambrose, and much as he insisted he had wanted to talk with him of his problems, could it be he did not really have the nerve to do so? Was he truly afraid of disturbing Ambrose's peace, or was he rather justifying a hidden fear that, should he realize the interview, he would probably have to hear things he was not yet prepared to hear?

The parallel with the psychological problems of innumerable people nowadays is striking! Does not the same kind of fear often take possession of them? Is it not next to impossible to help people who will not first admit that they really have a problem? that they need help? Such is certainly the case with alcoholics, drug addicts, habitual liars, and many others who appear to be very confused people. But there was another pitfall into which Augustine had frequently fallen in those years, a pitfall which still exists in our own times. On hearsay, he had condemned things of which he was really ignorant, including matters of interpretation of the Scriptures and the teaching of the Church. Experience has taught me that there are all too many good Catholics and Christians who do not know or understand what or why the Church teaches as it does.

Though Augustine claimed that he was dedicated to discovering the truth, his actions made it clear that he was not yet really open to learning. Moreover, the fact that in matters of faith and religion he insisted on having a certainty which could only be found in the field of mathematics also contributed to his being painfully shackled to his own ideas. Even at the age of thirty, after so many disappointments and according to his own testimony, he still held out hope of finding wisdom "to-morrow," all by himself! And unfortunately there are still those who think they can resolve all their problems, fears, and hang-ups by themselves, without any help from others.

Fourth Phase: Listening to God's Healing Word

But something new was also beginning to happen, and this was to be the final phase of Augustine's long journey. Through Ambrose, God's healing word was penetrating bit by bit to Augustine's heart. Because he had admitted his helplessness, his mind was finally open to real listening and his pride was diminishing, so that he became capable of see-ing the error of his ways. Still his strong passions led him to procrastinate. At the same time, however, he also found quiet moments for prayer and reflection, and little graces were mixed together with his sufferings, which gave him a new vi-sion of things. He listened to Simplicianus and Ponticianus, as one would to special teachers. He heard that people far greater than himself in the eyes of the world—as Victorinus—had given up everything for the faith. And most of all, he fi-nally began to know himself, to see himself as he really was, and no longer as he had dreamed he was. With this his pride was shattered and humility entered in. With a supreme effort, fortified by the special grace of God and washed by abundant tears of repentance, he snapped the bonds of his nagging pas-sions, and peace flooded his soul. What a grace for Augustine, as also for those who have similarly opened themselves to God's graces after the hesitations and the doubts of years of trial! What peace can flood the soul when it can finally sur-render itself and turn back to God after a short or prolonged separation! How great is God's love and mercy for all of us!

A Final Thought

God is still at work among his people today, as he was in the case of Augustine. God wills no one to be lost. In fact he would have us all be his friends as we grow in the two great commandments of his love. But in order to accomplish this, we really need to take Jesus' advice to change and become like little children. This challenge exists for all who seek true happiness. We need to turn away from what impedes our journey and accept God's teaching in all simplicity. We need to know ourselves and know God, know the truth and not run away from it or make excuses so as not to have to face it. We need to be open to seeking help and learning from others. Above all we have to really want to change or be renewed, and be prepared to do what is necessary to bring about this change or renewal in a serious way. Such is the path Augustine had to travel. It is the very path all must travel in searching for God, returning to him, clinging to him, growing in him, and receiving fullness of life from him.

5

Prayer: Knocking at God's Door with Persistence

"This is the house of our prayers," Augustine once said of a new church he was dedicating, "but we ourselves are the house of God" [S 336, 1]. What a magnificent summary of the beauty of our Christian faith in that short sentence: *We are the house of God.* And it makes good sense! If we are made in the image and likeness of God, if God has given us an inner eye by which we can find and see him, and if Christ is really the interior Master who enlightens us from within where he dwells, then truly we are God's house, a house that is continually in construction until the end of time, a house that grows and increases in beauty and value with every act of faith-filled love.

Though we sometimes gather to pray with fellow Christians as a community in the temple that is our local church, where the many offer worship to God with one heart and one voice, the very first temple which must be sanctified by prayer is this temple which is ourselves, the house of God. Augustine asks his people rather concisely:

> Do you want to sing psalms? Then let not your voice alone sound God's praises, but let your good works be in tune with your voice. When you sing with your voice, you will sometimes fall silent; sing with your life, then, so that you need never be silent [On Ps 146, 2].

Prayer Is an Attitude

The temple of the Lord, which is ourselves, must also be a place of prayer, that is, a place of communion with God, but not of such prayer or communion as relies only on words. Prayer must go together with good works, for the gospel makes it quite clear that we cannot be serious about praising or petitioning God if at the same time we neglect our neighbor. How we honor the house of God or the house of our prayer depends very much on our attitude toward the needy, the helpless, God's little ones.

On another occasion Augustine told his people that we go to the house of the Lord, not so much with our feet as with our affections [see On Ps 121, 11]. That's a quaint way of saying that if our hearts are not in our prayer, it hardly matters where our feet may have taken us or where the body may find itself; our prayer will have little, if any, value. Augustine himself gives us an example of how this can happen in his *Confessions*. He went off to college, some two hundred miles from home and away from his mother's influence. He was already losing interest in his childhood faith. Yet apparently habit still played a strong role in his life, for it kept him going to church, at least for a while. But his heart was evidently not in it.

> I abandoned you, Lord, to follow a sacrilegious curiosity that was going to cast me into the very depths of skepticism and into the deceitful worship of devils . . . Even in the celebration of Mass, within the very walls of your church, I dared to stir up impure thoughts and seek to satisfy them [Conf 3, 3].

So how can we be more sure that our hearts are in our prayers, that our prayer lives are healthy and ever more meaningful? Perhaps Augustine's mature reflections on these matters in what follows can be very helpful.

Prayer Is from the Heart

How does Augustine understand prayer? What did it mean to him? Far from being a mere duty or obligation, prayer for Augustine is essentially a longing or yearning, which arises from faith, a response, as it were, to God's speaking to us through revelation, through other people, through the particular circumstances of our lives, and especially through his Son. "When you read the Scriptures God speaks to you, but when you pray, you speak to God" [On Ps 85, 7]. Could it be any clearer that Augustine looks upon prayer not as a monologue but as a real dialogue, a response from the heart to God's call? Listen to what he says:

> When we pray to God, whether with words, when they are needed, or in silence, we must always cry out from the heart. This cry of the heart is a powerful impulse of the spirit which, when it happens in prayer, expresses the great affection of the one who prays and petitions, showing that there is no lack of trust to obtain what is being asked [On Ps 118: S 29, 1].

Though Augustine clearly indicates in this quote that there are times when we ought to pray in words, he also warned his people very explicitly lest at any time they merely mouth these words in sterile formulas, so to speak, and leave their hearts out of the whole process. That could be disastrous, and yet unfortunately this can still happen today, just as it did in the fifth century:

> How many there are who cry out with their words and are silent in their hearts! And on the other hand, how many say not a word and cry out with their love! The ear of God is attentive to the human heart. Just as the human ear listens to the mouth of a human being, so the ear of God listens to the human heart. Many are heard even though they keep their mouths closed, and many are not heard despite their thunderous cries [On Ps 119, 9].

Augustine understands prayer as the longing or desire of the heart to be united with what alone can satisfy our restlessness and give us that happiness we quite naturally seek. That object is none other than God, and that longing is nothing if not love:

> You do not yet see what you so much desire. But it is precisely by desiring it that you are made capable of being filled by it . . . By putting off that vision, [God] increases our desire for

it; by making us long for it, he stretches the soul and by stretching it he increases its capacity [On 1 John 4, 6].

Furthermore, each of us becomes what we love, says Augustine. If we love the earth, we will be earthy. If we love God—well, it is not I who would dare say it on my own authority, he adds, but the Scriptures do say it: "I said, you are gods and sons and daughters of the Most High" [On 1 John 2, 14].

Prayer is at one and the same time a response, a dialogue, and a loving desire of the heart. We give expression to it in words, in silence, and in our outgoing service to others. At the same time we do well to remember that it is not we who initiate the response or dialogue that is prayer. It is the Spirit of God dwelling within who moves us to prayer, who encourages us to pray, who intercedes for us, and who even interprets to the Father the real sense of our groaning in prayer:

The Spirit too helps us in our weakness, for we do not know how to pray as we ought; but the Spirit himself makes intercession for us with groanings that cannot be expressed in speech. He who searches hearts knows what the Spirit means, for the Spirit intercedes for the saints as God himself wills [Rom 8:26-27].

Augustine would say that the Spirit makes us search for the One we want to meet and call out to the One we want to reach. And because this One is no other than the Spirit of Jesus, promised by the Master himself, we can rightly say with Augustine: "[Jesus] prays for us as our priest; he prays in us as our head; and he is prayed to by us as our God" [On Ps 85, 1].

Prayer of Silence, Prayer Within

When Pope John Paul II was in Denver in the summer of 1993, he made a statement that attracted a lot of attention: "America needs much prayer, lest it lose its soul." What John Paul predicated of this country could easily be applied to many people—even good people—and also to other countries! One priest-author whom I read recently stated that the longest journey he had ever made was from his head to his heart. It took him fifty years, he said, and he was referring to his attitude toward prayer, or better, his manner of praying. I wonder if that is not true of many of us also? Prayer for all too many is still very much of a "head trip." It does not possess that simplicity, that interior element, which Augustine found so important if prayer is to lead us closer to God.

It might be helpful to insert here a personal experience. When I was in the seminary [between ages eighteen and twenty-six, and in the years before Vatican II], it was the prevalent opinion of spiritual writers and counselors that the prayer of contemplation was only for the very few, the "elect," as it were. We were told quite clearly that we should not even think about trying it ourselves, but should stick to the processes of meditation to which we had been introduced in those seminary years. As I remember those "processes," they were indeed mostly "head trips." I must admit, it took me a long time to realize that this kind of intellectual approach to prayer was getting me nowhere. It was also causing me to slack off on every kind of quiet prayer, for it all seemed so sterile. The Lord was good to me. After Vatican II I came in contact with a new way of thinking, which I found much more suited to my disposition: just sitting quietly before the Lord, not seeking to do or learn anything, but to open myself to what God might want from me, whenever he might be willing to show me his will, and in whatever circumstances. This is the basis of the type of prayer that has nourished me since then and has given me new insights into God's ways.

For Augustine, the key word in our search for God is "within." Our search for God and our prayer to God must begin "within." As he puts it: there we will find truth, light, joy, Christ himself. It is there we will be heard when we pray. It is there we will come to worship and love God [see Tack, 48]. I think this is exactly what John Paul was trying to say: It is not enough merely to "say" our prayers; we must learn to let them rise from the very depths of our being. When we do this, we are opening ourselves to the work of the Spirit within, we are disposing ourselves to listen, rather than to talk, we are relying on the obscure nature of faith, rather than on an understanding we have from reason alone.

There is a tremendous need for more silence in our lives. The old spiritual masters were right in insisting on silence in order to have a sharper ear for the interior voice of God. We are all too often surrounded by noise, both at home and at work (and on our way to and from work!). Many people seem to thrive on that external noise, but it is very hard to hear the Spirit in situations like that. One spiritual writer has expressed very beautifully what this inner silence is for us: "To sit in silence [in prayer] is to sit in our brokenness with total acceptance and to be drawn into the beauty of the silence of God" [Eastman, 3]. That thought is deserving of much reflection!

Augustine was very much aware of this beauty of the silence of God, so much so that it led him to advise his people that they should listen attentively, not just to his words as a preacher, but especially to the words of the Master, Jesus, who would speak within their hearts. What he implies is that God uses words, preaching, example, the reading of the Scripture, and whatever else to awaken in the hearts of each person what is most helpful for him or her. This inner Master is precisely the one who will enlighten us concerning the mysteries of our faith, the knowledge of God, the teachings of God's Church:

> Enter into your heart, and if you have faith, there you will find Christ. There he himself will speak to you. I raise my voice, but he teaches you better in silence. I speak through the words of a sermon. He speaks within through the fear he inspires in your thoughts . . . Because you have faith in your hearts, Christ dwells there also: he will teach you what I desire to proclaim with my word [S 102, 2].

> He is much more present to you than I am, for while I appear to your eyes, he presides over your consciences. Give me, then, your ears, but give him your hearts, so that you may fill both [On John 1, 7].

Fraternal Love Leads to Prayer

But though Augustine speaks clearly of the importance of interior prayer, of a prayer of silence, he never intended that we should in this way separate ourselves from the reality of everyday life. As a matter of fact he returns over and over again to a key idea when he states that the practice of fraternal love is one of the quickest ways of assuring that we reach God through prayer. It is by loving our brothers and sisters that we open our interior vision to seeing God: "By loving your neighbor you cleanse your eyes so that you can see God" [On John 17, 8]. Love of neighbor is the everyday reality to which we must all be sensitive. Augustine emphasizes this strongly in his *Rule,* where he is far more concerned about how his religious followers live together in harmony and unity, than about how they should pray, either as a community or individually. Dialogue with others in Augustine's mind is basic to discovering and honoring the presence of Christ in one another and in any kind of community or family. In fact, Augustine emphasizes this with these words from his *Rule:* "Live together then in oneness of mind and heart, mutually honoring God in yourselves, whose temples you have become" [I, 8]. It is not just religious or priests who are the temple of God; all of us are! To live a life of faith is to open ourselves to a life of prayer and to a better recognition of the presence of God in ourselves and in others.

Some Difficulties in Prayer

Prayer can be a very beautiful and satisfying experience for a person of faith. Yet there are a lot of apparent difficulties and misunderstandings about prayer which can make it quite a struggle. Many of these difficulties have been around a long time, so let us take a look at some of them.

Why pray at all if God knows all things? Will our prayer make God change his mind? Why use words when God does not need them to understand us? How can anyone pray all the time, as the gospel seems to imply? I think the basic answer to a lot of these normal difficulties lies in understanding once again the very nature of prayer as Augustine conceives it: it is a loving desire of the heart, directed toward God in response to what God has said and still does say to us through the Scriptures and through the many circumstances of our lives, positive or negative as they may be.

Since prayer of its very nature is a desire, a loving desire, it needs to be nourished like any other great desire in our lives. Otherwise it will fade away. Such a desire needs to be kept in the foreground and reflected upon, so that it can be better appreciated. And this must be done, no matter how difficult it may seem or how helpless we may feel in asking for certain things. The following story may help us understand how our prayer must be ours—personal, that is—and not just so many formal words.

Appreciating God's Gift of Prayer

When I was in Tanzania (East Africa) visiting our missionaries in a very remote part of this materially poor country, I saw how deprived the people were of many things we take for granted or consider necessary in life. The missionaries told me that many good Christians from their home country—Spain—had sent clothing and books and other useful articles to help these very needy people, yet at first the people had refused to accept these gifts. The missionaries were truly puzzled at this attitude until they found out why these gifts were being refused. Basically the people had two reasons: *first,* they felt that whatever did not cost anything could not really be of much value; *second,* their personal dignity would have been offended if they had had to accept items from foreigners without making any contribution themselves. This situation was quickly remedied: the missionaries put a nominal fee on all the articles (the equivalent of 5, 10, or 25 cents) and the people snapped them up. Everyone was happy, and the dignity of the people was safeguarded.

That story says a lot to me about prayer. If all we asked for were given to us on a silver platter, so to speak, it is most likely we would not really appreciate it. We would not have invested anything in it or at least not very much, and as a result, what we received would not really have much value for us. When children have to buy something for themselves with their own hard-earned money, they are more likely to appreciate it and take good care of it than were it simply given to them, especially if they had experienced no previous desire for the article. Students who have to help pay for some of their tuition in a private school or in college will also appreciate their education much more: they have had to earn it; it is not all free! Furthermore, turning our thoughts to God often merits a low priority rating in our lives, not only at times because of our own fault, but also because of the many distractions that are ours in having to attend to the material necessities of life. We need to remind ourselves frequently of the importance of God in our lives, we need to understand better what the important things are that we should be seeking, and we need to have a hand in seeking these things ourselves. This is the way our desires are sharpened and our appreciation is increased. And this is why prayer is so important.

Augustine has much to say about all these things in his letter to the Roman lady Proba, who had fled to Africa from Rome to get away from the violence of the invading Vandals. Here are a few remarks from that letter that we can all take to heart:

> (Our Lord and God) wishes our desires to be expressed in prayers so that we may be able to receive what he is ready to give . . . Hence words are necessary for us that we may be more alert and fully aware of what we are asking, but we are not to think that they are necessary so the Lord can be informed or influenced . . . We turn our mind to the task of prayer at appointed hours since that desire (for the happy life) grows lukewarm, so to speak, from our involvement in other concerns and occupations . . .
>
> Lengthy talk is one thing, a prayerful disposition which lasts a long time is another . . . Excessive talking should be kept out of prayer . . . (But) to spend much time in prayer is to knock with a persistent and holy fervor at the door of the one whose help we implore. This task is generally accomplished more through sighs than words, more through weeping than speech [L 130:9, 16–10, 20].

Prayer Changes Us, Not God

The words of our prayers—or even our interior groanings, prompted by the Spirit—make us much more aware of what we need. But they do not change God. That is why Augustine says that excessive talking is useless in prayer, but not a prayerful disposition. God is not going to change his mind toward us. His basic disposition will always be one and the same: that of love, which desires to unite us to himself, even when we turn away from him. But we ourselves can and do change. Precisely because our interior dispositions change, we may seem to find God "changed" in a certain way. In much the same way, when our eyes have become very sensitive due to inflammation, the light of the sun seems harsh instead of mild, irritating instead of pleasant, and yet the sun has not changed at all; only our relationship to it is altered because of something that is going on in our own lives [see City 22, 2, 1]. Prayer does change us, and that is why one author who writes on Augustine can state:

> Words are used, not to stir God to action, nor to persuade him to comply with our wishes, but rather to stir up in us an awareness of and desire for the things we ought to seek. In other words language in prayer serves to remind us of our Christian ideals and helps to mold our desires accordingly. Its purpose is to change us, not God [Corcoran 24].

Instant Answers

A much greater difficulty than those we have been talking about lies in considering why our prayers are not answered with greater urgency, especially when it is so evident that we are asking for good things, either for ourselves or for others. This problem has been around for centuries. But it is probably more troublesome to us today because of what we have grown to expect in almost every area of life.

We live in times of instant response: we have instant food (coffee, tea, TV dinners); instant communication over long distances by phone, fax, or e-mail; instant Polaroid photos and photocopies of documents; instant correction of our mistakes on our computers; instant pleasure at the flick of a switch or the press of a button. So quite naturally we have great difficulty understanding a lack of instant response to our prayers. We hate to be left in suspense, to have to wait in long lines. People in the former Eastern block countries of

Europe, where long lines had been an everyday fact of life under Communism, probably have a lot more patience in waiting for things than we do. They waited for almost everything and never knew if they would find it still in supply when they reached the end of the line. We most often wait, not for the necessities of life, but for more pleasurable items: a pleasant vacation, a long-expected visit, tickets to a special ball game.

Augustine once reminded his people that not even St. Paul had his prayer answered as he desired. After Paul had incessantly prayed that a certain affliction be removed from him, the Lord told him: "My grace is sufficient for you, for strength is made perfect in weakness" [2 Cor 12:9]. Why was his petition not heard, Augustine asks rhetorically? Because it would not have been good for him! His desire was not granted so that what was good for him could be granted. God's beloved ones are always heard when it is a matter of what is really good for us, especially for our eternal salvation, because in the depths of our hearts that is what we are really praying for when we ask for anything. Augustine then applied this to his listeners:

> If God does not grant what we desire, he will always grant us what is for our good. What would happen if you were to ask the doctor for what he knew would be harmful for you? . . . Do you think he was not listening to you because he did not give you what you wanted? Quite the contrary, he heard you while looking out for your health, for what was really good for you . . . Learn how to ask God for what he, the doctor, knows to be good for you. Tell him your illness, but let him apply the remedy [On 1 John 6, 8].

God Knows What Is Best

I have had quite a few mothers tell me how heart-broken they have been because their sons or daughters have fallen away from the Church and no longer practice the faith in which they were raised with such love by their parents. These mothers are at a loss as to what they should do. And they wonder out loud how it is that God can allow their children to wander so far from the truth, how it can be that God does not grant their prayers, when what they are asking for is evidently so very right and good. When I hear this line of questioning, my mind runs right to the situation that developed between Augustine and his mother Monica, which is very similar to what these mothers are going through.

Monica felt totally frustrated when Augustine first went off to the University of Carthage, took a mistress for himself and, worst of all, joined up with the Manichees. Monica's instinctive reaction—which I am sure is the case with many other mothers—was to throw Augustine out of the house, to refuse to eat with him. However, after she had had time to rethink her position, she relented and welcomed him back to both house and table. But that did not change Augustine one little bit! It even gave him the bold confidence to tell his mother that one day she would join him in this sect, because he was right and she was wrong! But Monica took a new approach: she began to pray with groans and tears for the conversion of her son. She prayed that way for thirteen years, and do not think she did not feel at a total loss as to why God apparently was not answering her prayers. Faith alone kept her going because she was confident that God would answer in his own time and way.

After about ten years in the Manichean sect and finding that they could no longer satisfy his needs, Augustine decided to go off to Rome and leave his mother behind in Africa. This he did, but he was only able to separate himself from her by deceit. This is how he writes about it in his *Confessions:*

> That very night I secretly set out on my journey, while she stayed behind praying and weeping. And what was she asking of you, my God, with so many tears if not that you would keep me from sailing away? But in the depth of your wisdom you did not listen to what she was asking at that moment. Rather you responded to the very heart of her petition, so that you might do for me what she had always asked of you . . . That very morning she was wild with grief and she filled your ears with moaning and groaning. But you paid no attention to these things. Rather you took advantage of my desires to draw me where I would put an end to these desires. And you allowed her to suffer the consequences of her too jealous love.

As is the custom with mothers—and her custom more than that of many others—she loved to have me at her side. As a result, she could not imagine how much happiness you were going to bring her through my separation from her [Conf 5, 8].

While this is a fascinating narrative, it also teaches us some deep theology. God did not give Monica everything she asked, because he had in mind to grant what was for her son's—and her own—greater good, that which was far more important! Monica's desire that he remain in Africa was not granted, so that through his contacts in Rome and Milan, Augustine might indeed find his way back to the Catholic faith. In hindsight both Monica and Augustine could see that. Neither could see it at the moment about which Augustine writes. And so it is frequently with us and our good desires: these are not always granted—even though they may be very good—because God is looking out for the total good of his people, not just for lesser desires which do not always allow for long-range effects. Furthermore, God will not destroy our free will: rather he will use that free will to lead us to himself, if only we will be open to the truth. "Your Father will give you only what he knows is advantageous for you. You know what you want; he knows what is good for you" [S 80, 2].

We owe, however, at least this much in our duty to God: if he does not take affliction away, we must not imagine that we are being forgotten by him but, because of our loving endurance of evil, must await greater blessings in its place. In this way, power shines forth more perfectly in weakness [L 130, 14, 26].

All too many people in our society do not understand the true nature of prayer, do not understand that there are different ways of praying, do not understand that it is essentially the Spirit dwelling within who invites us to prayer and carries our response to God, interpreting to the Father what we really want, what is most important for us. We who do pray, who have a great desire for drawing closer to God and carrying out his holy will, must be witnesses to the joy of real prayer and to how our prayers will be answered in God's time, and always for our greater good. Since Jesus does pray in us as our head, we must do all we can to keep this temple, this house of the Lord which is ourselves, holy and without blemish or stain in his sight.

6

He Was Lost and Has Been Found: Celebrating God's Mercy

We Had To Celebrate and Rejoice!

One of the most moving passages of the New Testament is chapter 15 of St. Luke's Gospel. The entire chapter is a personification of the great mercy of God and an expression of the profound joy God experiences when a sinner returns to him. There Jesus tells us three parables, each of which offers a tremendous message of hope and love to those who have erred or have even lost their way through life: the parables of the lost sheep, the lost coin, and the lost, or prodigal, son. At the conclusion of the first two parables, Jesus emphasizes what great joy there is in heaven over the repentance of just one sinner. This same joy is manifested in a somewhat different, but much more powerful, way by the prodigal son's father when he says: "But we had to celebrate and rejoice! This brother of yours was dead, and has come back to life. He was lost, and is found" [Luke 15:32].

There is an air of great urgency in these words, which make it clear that no other course of action was possible; what else could that father do in such circumstances but celebrate? It was such a marvelous thing that this boy should return home after such a miserable life of sin, that his father and the whole family had to show their happiness in gratitude for what had happened. Finding a lost sheep or a silver coin is certainly very important to its owner, especially when that person is poor or of very modest means. But Jesus takes pains to show us just how much more important to God is the recovery of one errant son or daughter. These images of our heavenly Father's tender compassion, mercy, and love, mingled with his great happiness at the return of one who was lost, cannot help but fill us also with gratitude, consolation, and a well-founded confidence that the same mercy will be extended to us, not necessarily because we have been lost and found again, but rather because we have been cleansed of our many failings and sins through sincere repentance and love, through reconciliation and the Eucharist.

Augustine was powerfully struck by these passages of the gospel. Because of his own wanderings and sins he had no trouble seeing himself in that prodigal son. In fact, on not a few occasions in his *Confessions,* Augustine refers this parable to himself. As we already saw above in chapter 4, Augustine had gone far astray before being called back by a special grace to totally embrace Christ and the Church. It was this personal experience of God's mercy and forgiveness that allowed him to be so persuasive as a bishop in urging his people to turn away from sin and wavering and to accept God's love and mercy.

What Augustine has to say to his people on this subject, both in some homilies and in other writings, can easily be applied to us today also. It applies to those who are sincerely striving to draw closer to God, as well as to those still struggling with some serious problems that keep them away from God or at least away from that desired intimacy with God. There is no one who is not in need of God's mercy, understanding, and compassion. Even after his baptism Augustine viewed conversion as an ongoing necessity in his own life. This spirit of conversion kept him open, so that he might always turn more completely toward God, who throughout his life continued to call and invite him to resemble more closely his Son, Jesus Christ.

Augustine used these very same images to speak to the hearts of his people, to touch them profoundly and call them back should they have strayed into the path of sin after baptism [see On Ps 77, 24]. Conversion was such a marvelous grace for Augustine that he did not hesitate to say that it was an even more wonderful thing than being raised from the dead. Here are some striking examples of how he communicated these ideas to his people:

> Every time we see mercy shown toward those who were lost and toward evil people brought to justification, what do we praise but the marvels of God? You praise the fact that the dead have risen, but it is more praiseworthy that lost men and women have been saved. What a grace, what a mercy of God! You see a person who was yesterday totally given over to drunkenness, and who today is an image of sobriety. You see one who was yesterday in the depths of impurity, and who today is clothed with temperance. You see one who yesterday cursed God, and who today praises him. You see one who was yesterday a servant of his own creatureliness, and today he worships his Creator. Yes, people have been converted from all these hopeless cases, but let them not think this is due to their own merits [On Ps 88: S 1, 6].

Conversion Is for Now

But while all this illustrates the great mercy of God toward the penitent sinner, Augustine was quick to remind his people that such repentance and conversion must take place in this life, not in the next; then it will be too late. No defense will then be possible for one who has procrastinated. There is proof of this, he adds, in the story of the rich man who died after having refused to give even the scraps from his table to the poor beggar, Lazarus, who sat at his doorstep:

> The soul also understands that now is the time for conversion. When this life shall have passed away, there will be nothing else but recompense for one's deeds . . . That rich man of whom the Lord speaks praised God in hell . . . but it did him no good, even though he did still admit that those punishments were afflicting him justly [On Ps 6, 6; see also On Ps 74, 14].

In Augustine's time, as in our own, there were people who believed there would always be another day in their

lives, a tomorrow, in which they could take care of necessary
repentance. After all, they would reason, ours is a God of
mercy and compassion. Will he not forgive us when we ask
him? For these people the good bishop had some very sage
advice, which might well be summed up in modern expression as: Forgiveness, yes! Tomorrow, not necessarily!

> God is indeed very patient in putting up with you now, but
> that does not mean that he will fail to be just in punishing
> . . . Do not say then: Tomorrow I shall be converted, tomor-
> row I shall please God, and all that I have done wrong today
> and yesterday will be forgiven me. What you say is true: God
> has promised forgiveness if you turn back to him. But what
> he has not promised is that you will have tomorrow in which
> to achieve your conversion [On Ps 144, 11].

Some Obstacles to Conversion

At the same time that Augustine communicates to us a
great sense of urgency concerning repentance and conversion, he is also very understanding of the difficulties that can
get in the way of achieving such a return to the Father, or
that can get in the way of growing in our relationship or
friendship with him.

What are some of the obstacles that can keep us from returning to God or drawing closer to him? The most important is certainly our sinfulness, especially that sinfulness
which has become habitual and burdensome, which seems
to drag us ever further down into ourselves and therefore
away from God. Such had been Augustine's experience, and
in his *Confessions* he gives dynamic expression to the conflict that so often arises in the very depths of our being in
such a situation:

> But I keep falling under the weighty burdens of this life. Habit
> ties me down and holds me back. I weep abundantly, but still
> I am held back, so strong is the burden of habit. Where I am
> fit to stay, I do not want to stay. Where I want to be, I am not
> fit to be. In both cases I find myself miserable [Conf 10, 40].

As Augustine tells us, we are really our own worst enemies. We do not want anything bad to happen to our mate-

rial goods or possessions, but it seems we are not nearly so careful about what affects our deeper, spiritual values. In this regard we often treat ourselves very poorly [see S 232, 8]!

However, probably the most serious problem that confronts those who want to turn over a new leaf, or simply draw closer to Christ, is the one that affected Augustine himself throughout his youth: pride! This pride can take on any number of shapes or forms. It can close our minds to hearing the truth from others. It can make us believe that we are capable of doing everything by ourselves, even with regard to attaining eternal happiness with God. It can literally make us believe we are a light to ourselves, or it can be responsible for afflicting us with an unforgiving nature. Augustine even mentions that he had been affected by a "blind belligerence" in his attitude toward the Catholic Church, an attitude which for many years cut him off from discovering the truth [see Conf 6, 3]. And so he could say to his people in summing up the terrible effects of pride:

> If you could be enlightened by yourself, you would never be in the dark, because you are always with yourself . . . Do not believe that you are a light to yourself. The Light is that which enlightens everyone coming into this world [On Ps 25: S 2, 11].

> Those who seem to themselves to be fully satisfied, though they are really starving; and those who seem to be full, though they are exceptionally empty, are not converted [On Ps 67, 31].

One of the more serious forms of pride is a failure to want to forgive those who have hurt us. This is often more harmful to a person's relationship with God than he or she is willing to admit. It is very difficult for some otherwise good Christians to forgive, yet that is a basic condition for our being forgiven and welcomed into our Father's house:

> Forgive, that you may be forgiven. In doing this, nothing is required of the body . . . it is the will that acts . . . You will experience no physical pain, you will have nothing less in your home. Now in truth, my brothers and sisters, you see how evil it is that one who has been commanded to love even his enemy does not pardon a penitent brother or sister [S 210, 10].

On the other hand, pride can also get in the way of our asking forgiveness when it is we who have hurt someone, and this too keeps us from full communion with the Lord and demands our "turning back":

> How many there are who know that they have sinned against their brothers or sisters and yet are unwilling to say: "Forgive me." They were not ashamed to sin, but they are ashamed to ask pardon; they were not ashamed of their evil act, but they blush where humility is concerned [S 211, 4].

Though pride is a major obstacle to our turning back to God or drawing closer to him, there are certainly many other obstacles which can make total conversion a difficult process: passion, greed, self-righteousness, complacency, excessive search for temporal pleasure, power, prestige, and many others. One other particular stumbling block I would like to mention in passing is that which ties many down to mediocrity or even to superficiality in their relations with God: the lack of good example, or better, the bad example itself which they receive from those who claim to be Christians and simply are not what they claim to be. Others may appear to be giving good example by frequently going to church, but they contradict themselves when they tear down their neighbor in the next breath.

Turning Around

The conversion of a sinner—just as the making of a saint—is a truly marvelous feat of divine providence, which rightly fills us with awe and gratitude. Conversion or growth in holiness would be unthinkable if God were not the infinitely good and merciful Father Jesus teaches us to love more than to fear. God is without doubt the principal agent in any conversion or growth in his love. But we ourselves also have essential roles to play. And yes, there are also others who can facilitate these movements toward God: the priest and other good Christians, especially those who have more direct contact with us. Finally, it is the entire Christian community which is called to rejoice with those who are reconciled or renewed, and who are called also to feel the pain of those who still live in mediocrity, without enthusiasm, or who continue to stray far afield. In many of his sermons Augustine brings out the varying roles of these four agents: God, the human person, the priest, and the Christian community. What Augustine has to say about conversion can also often be applied to those who are struggling to overcome their human weakness and draw nearer to God. There is something here for all of us.

1. GOD ALWAYS ACTS FIRST

What is God's role in conversion? Augustine knew that role first hand from his own conversion and he praised God continually for this grace in his *Confessions* [see Conf 10, 27]. He carried this experience over to his preaching, as he points out to his people that it is a pure gift of God's that we are called back to him. God does not treat us as we deserve, but in keeping with his great mercy. He draws us, heals us, changes us, makes us good, and fills us with his blessings in ever so many ways, despite past unfaithfulness on our part. If he were not to take the initiative and follow through, we would be lost:

> What is there to say, then? Did you make it possible for yourself to merit God's mercy because you turned back to him? . . . If you had not been called, what could you have done to turn back? Did not the very one who called you when you were turned away from him make it possible for you to turn back? Do not claim your conversion as your own doing, then, because unless God had called you when you were running away from him, you would not have been able to turn back [On Ps 84, 8].

> It is God who justifies the one who turns to him, and admonishes the one who is still far away so that he may be converted . . . [On Ps 58: S 2, 2].

> The One who has given us the gift of being gives us also the gift of being good. He gives to those who have turned back to him. Did he not even seek them out before they were converted, and when they were far from his ways? [On Ps 103: S 4, 2].

But how does God call us to conversion or to a greater holiness of life? What are the means he usually employs? Normally God uses very ordinary means, available to everyone; the extraordinary are rare, and really they are not necessary:

> No matter where you look, [God] calls us to correct ourselves and invites us to do penance: he calls through the wonderful gifts of his creation, he calls by granting us time for life, he calls us through the lector and through the preacher, he calls us with the innermost force of our thoughts, he calls with the scourge of punishment, and he calls us with the mercy of his consolation [On Ps 102, 16].

God's activity, then, in bringing us to our senses is manifold. He is never absent from us, and he never turns away from us; it is rather "our turning away which has caused us to lose him" [On Ps 6, 5]. To drive home this point to his listeners, Augustine appeals to that very imagery of the lost sheep and the prodigal son with which we began these considerations:

> For though the sheep could lose itself while wandering under its own power, it could not find itself, nor would it have been found, if the mercy of the shepherd had not sought it out. The prodigal son also belongs to this sheepfold, for when he came to his senses, he said: "I shall rise up and go to my father." By a hidden call and inspiration he too was sought out and raised up by that one who gives life to all things. And by whom was he found, if not by that one who came to save and search out what was lost? [On Ps 77, 24].

2. BUT IT IS WE WHO RESPOND

If such is the great mercy of God, would it not seem to be best just to sit back and leave everything completely in his hands, without making any effort ourselves? What a tragic mistake that would be! It is true: God created us without consulting us, but he will certainly not save us without our cooperation [see S 169, 13]. That being the case, our work is cut out for us, just as Augustine says:

> Your first task is to be dissatisfied with yourself, fight sin, and transform yourself into something better. Your second task is to

put up with the trials and temptations of this world which will
be brought on by the change in your own life, and to persevere
to the very end in the midst of these things [On Ps 59, 5].

To fight sin, put up with temptations, be transformed, and
persevere to the end are not, however, tasks that we can accomplish by ourselves. This is very clear from what we have
seen already concerning the mercy and initiative of God in
our regard. When we cry out to him for help in the trials of
this life, then, he expects us to have our priorities straight: he
does not want us to be pleading with him for temporal blessings when more importantly we should be asking for that
conversion which will bring us to eternal life [see On Ps 21,
S 3]. Augustine comments on his own conversion by reminding us that it is by humble prayer that we return to God,
are cleansed of past evil, and share in his mercy. It is through
such a prayer that God mercifully hears the groans of those
tied down by sin and frees them from their self-made chains
[see Conf 3, 8].

Yet despite the fact that God encourages and gently prods
us with his grace, how very difficult is the entire process of
conversion! Bad habits and confused priorities can and often
do weigh us down and create obstacles, either to our return
to God, or to our desire to draw closer to him. If we really
want to be healed and make progress, we must turn to the
Lord with confidence:

When we transform our old way of life and give our spirit a
new image, we find it very hard and painful to turn back from
the darkness of earthly passions to the serene calm of the divine light. It is in such perplexities that we say: "Turn, O Lord,"
that is, help us so that a complete conversion may be brought
about in us, a conversion that finds you ready to offer yourself
for the enjoyment of those who love you [On Ps 6, 5].

Prayer and humility are key elements in receiving this
grace, just as a closed mind and pride are key obstacles to
achieving repentance and conversion. But prayer and humility must be joined by a firm determination to fight against
whatever impedes progress, and that also means knowing how

to make our bodies serve the whole person and not just their particular pleasures: "If you wish so to fight that you do not merely beat the air, but strike your opponent manfully, then chastise your body and bring it into subjection . . ." [S 216, 6].

As I mentioned above in chapter 3, Augustine was accustomed to offer a special exhortation to the newly baptized who were going back to their secular activities, urging them to "follow the example only of those who are striving to lead good lives." The same advice, however, was equally valid for all who were sincerely striving to turn their lives around or draw closer to God. All were urged to choose wisely those Christians they would imitate: "Seek the good; hold fast to the good; be good yourselves" [S 223, 1]!

Finally, Augustine put his people on their guard against an error common to his own times, and repeated frequently in our times: the belief that small sins and failings are inconsequential. Concerning these smaller sins, Augustine tells us, God has given us daily remedies to provide for our purification, among which the Lord's Prayer itself occupies a very special place. He urges us to use this particular God-given remedy with sincerity, and not to let these smaller sins weigh us down by their sheer numbers:

> Let us say, and let us say with sincerity, because it is an alms in itself: "Forgive us our debts, as we also forgive our debtors." . . . But how can sins be called trifling if they oppress and bury us? What is more minute than drops of rain? Yet they fill the rivers. What is more minute than grains of wheat? Yet they fill the barns. You note the fact that they are rather small, but you do not note that there are many of them. You know how to take note of that fact that they are small; well, then, count too if you can. Still God has certainly given us a daily remedy [S 261, 10].

The point Augustine seems to be making is that conversion is not simply a once-in-a-lifetime affair for those who have drifted far away. Rather, it constitutes an ongoing attitude by which we search for and turn constantly to God, even in the midst of minor, daily falls.

3. GOD'S MINISTER APPEALS

God's minister, the priest, often has a very thankless task to perform. He must frequently call, plead, and exhort fellow Christians to be mindful of their dignity, repent, and turn from sin and injustice back to God. He must urge them to fight the good fight and persevere to the end. Oftentimes he must appear, both to himself and to others, to be something of a "broken record" (or like a worthless song, as a more literal translation of Augustine's text might put it). Such a "broken record" not only grates on one's ears and nerves, but it is also very little appreciated:

> What shall I do? I have become like a "broken record," begging you: "Change yourselves, change yourselves." The end of life is uncertain. Everyone walks about at his own risk . . . Are you planning on a long life, and do not fear sudden death? . . . Before God I rend my garments! I am afraid of being accused for not having spoken out. I shall fulfill my duty, seeking what is good for you. I want to rejoice because of your good works, not because of your money . . . My wealth is nothing if your hope is not in Christ . . . I beseech you, my brothers and sisters, if you are mindful of yourselves, have pity on me [S 232, 8]!

The fact that, all else failing, Augustine should appeal to the compassion of his people for himself is a sure sign of the close bond that must have united him with them, something which all ministers would do well to imitate. Moreover, this appeal to compassion is the same approach he uses on another occasion, in his *Rule* for religious, in order to provide the brothers and sisters with still another reason for obeying their superiors willingly. Love is at the root of that compassion, sincere love for the superior, or in this case the preacher, and a real appreciation of the burden he carries for the rest of us.

And yet the priest especially, through his ministry of preaching, must keep up his good efforts, in season and out, in the confident assurance that a fundamental conversion is always possible in this life. He must continue to warn his people of the dangers they face; he must also encourage

them constantly to trust in the Lord, imitate those who strive
to lead good lives, and never give up hope:

> On this threshing floor, in truth, grain can degenerate into
> chaff; and on the other hand, the chaff can be turned back
> into grain. These changes take place daily, my brothers and
> sisters. This life is full of afflictions and consolations. Daily
> those who seemed good fall and perish; and again, those who
> seemed evil are converted and live. For "God does not will
> the death of the sinner, but only that he be converted from his
> ways and live" [S 223, 2].

Not everyone wants to hear appeals to do good such as
these, not even when they are offered out of love; some will
continue in their obstinacy to the very end. In one of his
commentaries on the psalms, Augustine deals with just such
a situation:

> It often happens that one tries to correct certain depraved
> and dishonest people who are under his care, but every effort
> and concern is useless. They are incorrigible, so we have to
> put up with them . . . On the other hand, this incorrigible
> person . . . is already in the Church . . . So what will you
> do? Where will you go? How will you separate yourself from
> these situations so as not to be burdened by them any longer?
> Listen: be as close to him as you can: speak to him, exhort,
> coax, threaten, correct him [On Ps 54, 8].

And if not even this works? Augustine shows himself
very philosophical about this whole issue; no doubt he must
have had plenty of experience with such individuals. In that
case, he says, you have nothing left but your suffering. Of
course, that too will help to mold the Christian by uniting
him or her more closely to the suffering of Christ.

4. THE CHURCH ENCOURAGES

Though God and the sinner have the principal roles to
play in the drama of conversion, the entire Church is also intimately involved in this work. Some members of the Church
are perhaps in a position to contribute to this process in some
of those same areas already indicated as belonging principally
to God's ministers. But what specifically can be expected of all

Christians? What should we all be doing so as to help our struggling brothers and sisters achieve the full effects of conversion or draw nearer to God, as they may sincerely desire?

Augustine appeals above all to the love of those who are trying to lead good Christian lives themselves. These people can provide first of all their own encouraging example. But they can also draw closer to those in need, showing them mercy and understanding. They can stir up the spiritually lukewarm or cold with their own enthusiasm, while recognizing in them the suffering Christ. Christ does not need our help himself. It is his followers who need our help, especially those who are down and out, spiritually or even materially, so they can find encouragement in what is often an uphill battle: "You who are fervent in spirit, be enkindled with the fire of love. Let your lives glow with the praises of God and irreproachable morals. One person is hot, another cold. Let the one who is hot warm the one who is cold" [S 234, 3].

Rejoicing in the Lord

Who can properly explain to another what it means to find the faith after a long search? Or what it means to come back to the welcoming arms of the Church after a prolonged absence? Who understands best what it means to have sins forgiven that have been weighing us down and to be able to start life anew with a clean slate? Or what it means to consecrate oneself to God by a solemn pact and thus set out on a life of following and imitating Christ more closely? Or again what it means to break out of a confining routine and be more generous than ever before? Who, indeed, but one who has personally lived such an experience!

Each of these examples is a type of conversion, which brings with it tremendous joy and peace of heart. Each invites the recipient of such a grace to love and praise God more generously and to thank him more sincerely for all the good things he has granted. Quite truthfully we can all say with the Psalmist: "The favors of the LORD I will sing forever" [Ps 89:2]. God's mercy knows no bounds in this life.

If it is true that the Father in heaven rejoices more over the return of one sinner than over ninety-nine others who are just, it is also true that the joy in the person who has received this great grace is without measure. Such a person can no longer be satisfied only with himself. His light, peace, and happiness are only in God:

> And now I return, parched and panting, to your fountain. Let no one keep me away from it, so that I may drink and have life. Let me not give life to myself, for on my own I have only lived evilly: I was death to myself, but in you I live renewed [Conf 12, 10].

At the end of life, when we shall all come before our Father in judgment, it is a consoling thought to know that our past failings and sins—small or great as they may have been—will not be there to impede our happiness, because they will have all been wiped away in reconciliation by the mercy of that loving Father. It is only his mercy that saves us now and brings us closer to him. It will only be his mercy that will reward us then with the gift of himself. "In you, O Lord, have I hoped; I shall never be disappointed" [*Te Deum,* final strophe].

7

Your Priest Is Only Human

The priesthood is an essential part of the Christian Catholic life. At the Last Supper Jesus ordained his apostles and gave them the power to offer the Eucharist in his memory. After his resurrection Jesus told them to go and preach the good news, and then he gave them the authority to forgive sins, or to withhold that forgiveness. From the side of Christ on the Cross, through the working of the Holy Spirit, and from the understanding of the Apostles as to what Jesus expected of them, the Church was born, which was to be the gathering of all the faithful in the name of Jesus. The priest then is called to be a special leader in the faith among his people, to be a minister of the Word and the Sacrament as Augustine puts it. He preaches, teaches, and sanctifies in the name of the Lord.

But what is, or what should be, the relationship of the priest with his people? This relationship has varied over the centuries, but the priest has always occupied a special place in the eyes of the Christian people. At times that place has been exaggerated. I remember growing up in the 1930s and 1940s and looking upon priests as almost superhuman. Along with many other Catholics of the era, I mentally put them on a pedestal. In the first ten or twelve years of my life, I probably never even dreamed that they had once been boys like myself, growing up in a normal family environment. Even when I came to realize they had grown up like any other normal person, I think I still put them on some kind of pedestal. I could not imagine them with weaknesses such as I or other people experienced. I could not understand anyone criticizing them. As a matter of fact, criticism of priests seemed to be very muted, if it existed at all in my youth. And then I grew up. I came to realize how human the priest was and what an injustice was done to him by those who expected him to be perfect.

If such a condition of distancing between pastor and people may have existed in past decades, perhaps especially before Vatican II, it is hard to imagine how such situations could exist today. It would be bad for both the priest and his people. The priest would not be able to know how his people were really thinking, and the Christian people would rightly feel neglected, frustrated in their attempts to form a living Christian community with him. Augustine certainly was not on any pedestal in relation to his people. In fact his rapport with his people was intense and close, no matter their background or academic preparation. It would seem to me that the manner in which Augustine related to his people and they to him is still quite applicable to the relationship that exists today between the priest and his people.

At Ease With All His People

For the most part Augustine's people were very simple, without too much education: fishermen, local merchants, those who had purchased their freedom from slavery. There were also among them, of course, the few well educated and wealthy, the leaders of the city and region, some high-ranking army officers, some businessmen, and eventually some others of importance, who came to Hippo Regius as refugees from Rome after it was invaded by the Vandals. Many of the citizens of this North African seaport city were people without any faith, or recent converts to the faith. Among the latter were those also who brought their former superstitious practices with them to their new religion. But with all—men and women alike—Augustine seemed to find himself perfectly at ease—and they with him. And this was true even though he frequently had to remind them forcefully of their duties to God, to one another, and to themselves. Augustine even bent over backward, so to speak, to try to reach the dissidents in his community—mainly those of the Donatist sect—and with many of their lay members he was quite successful.

This rapport is nothing less than remarkable, especially considering the prestigious education Augustine had received, his former influential position in the court of the emperor in Milan, and his ever-growing reputation as a brilliant defender of the very faith he had once fought against, much as St. Paul had done.

How was it possible for him to be on such good terms with so diverse a population? Probably many factors contributed, not the least being the hard lesson of humility which he had learned over the long years in which his fierce pride had kept him from the Church. Like St. Paul before his conversion, that pride had actually made him a dangerous enemy of the Church, who won many converts to the Manichean way of life when he was a Manichee himself. Another factor was that Augustine himself had come from a small town in the hinterland of what is present-day Algeria, a town named Thagaste, where most likely everybody knew everybody else, and there was little pretension among the people. A third, and perhaps the most compelling reason for Augustine's closeness with the people was, without doubt, that he clearly understood his mission as priest and bishop, and what the Lord expected of one in such a position of responsibility. Apparently he communicated this awareness to his people in word and work.

Quite likely the majority of priests today do not come from small towns, as Augustine did. But whether from small towns or large cities, there is no reason why relationships between today's priests and their people should not imitate Augustine's openness, especially through the practice of sincere humility and a better understanding of their mission. At the same time the fulfillment of this goal does not depend solely on the priests, but also on the Lord, though the Lord rightly expects of his priests a great amount of prayer, simplicity, and love in seeking this humility and understanding.

Trust in God Alone!

The Christians of Hippo loved their pastor, and he very evidently loved them. He understood quite well their practical strengths and weaknesses, which was a great advantage in being able to teach and confirm them in the faith. The people on their part were fiercely proud of him as their spiritual leader. Many flocked to listen to him, hung on his every word, and stood sometimes for as much as an hour or two while he preached, something that today almost all of us would find quite annoying, to put it mildly. They emoted with him and would applaud enthusiastically [as was the custom in Africa in those times] in order to express agreement with something he said that particularly appealed to them. And they did all this even though he pulled no punches when it was necessary to be critical of certain of their practices, which he considered inconsistent with the Christian faith [e.g., their boisterous parties on feast days, which were the occasion for much public drinking, drunkenness, and riotousness].

Yet this close relationship with the people was also an occasion of concern for him. He not only feared becoming a victim of pride once again because of their frequent praise, but he also feared for their spiritual good, that is, that his people would end up putting more trust in him, or in any other popular minister, than in the Lord. Augustine knew very well that this could only lead to disaster—to a cult of personality, which was then and is still now totally unacceptable for a Catholic priest, bishop, or religious who claims to represent the humble Christ. Here is an example of how he spoke to his people about this problem:

> It is our Chief Shepherd himself who has warned us . . . to refrain from putting our trust even in [good shepherds], to refrain from setting our hopes on them because of their good works; rather, he tells us, we ought to give glory to him who has made them this way, to the Father who is in heaven (Matt 5:16) [L 208, 4].

Whatever we are, let not your trust be in us . . . If I find people putting their trust in me, I do not congratulate them. They are to be corrected, not encouraged; changed, not affirmed . . . Do not let your hopes rest on us, do not let your hopes rest on men . . . Insofar as we are good, we will be faithful ministers, truly ministers [S 340A, 9].

There are perhaps several reasons why Augustine warned his people not to put their trust in him but in God, the author of all good things, reasons which are still valid for our times. First, any real honor and praise rightly belong only to God, as is clear from the gospel message of Jesus. Second, even good ministers must share with others, not what is their own, but what they have received. Therefore, when they preach and teach they are doing nothing exceptional; it is their sacred duty, which they dare not neglect, even though it means speaking up about unpopular topics, like sin, the cross, injustice in the market place, things that go against the grain. It is a strange kind of pastor that would fear to speak out about unpleasant things and only want to speak to his people about the joy of being friends with God or about earthly happiness [see S 46]. Third, though the vast majority of ministers in the Church are good, dedicated men, there may also be some few who have made themselves unworthy of their call. As the Lord has taught us, we must do as they teach, without imitating their lives. Yet while the people willingly listen to those who give good example, they may be quite unwilling to listen to those who do not, or who, worse yet, may even be leading lives that are anything but exemplary. Augustine comments on just such a situation, which must have existed in his own time, making a distinction between the way the good-living and the bad-living often react in these situations:

So when the laity who want to lead good lives pay attention to a bad priest, what do they say to themselves? . . . "We must hear from him the words that are not his own, but God's. We must follow God; let this man follow his own desires." . . . But as for the laity who are bad and unfaithful . . . what do they say to themselves when God's word censures them? "Go away: why speak to us? If not even bishops and priests do what you tell them to do, then why are you compelling us to do so?" They are not seeking an advocate for themselves in a bad cause, but a companion in punishment . . . [S 137, 7].

Salvation can certainly be preached by those who are without salvation themselves, by those, that is, who, though ordained ministers, are at heart only menial opportunists. There were apparently some in Augustine's time, which made him put his people especially on guard:

> There are people in the Church . . . who preach the gospel with the desire to receive a reward of whatever sort, seeking not so much the salvation of those to whom they preach as their own advantage. But those who hear salvation from the lips of one who is himself without salvation must believe in the One about whom he is preaching, without placing their hope in that person through whom salvation is being preached to them [S 137, 5].

Pay Attention to the Content, Not to the Wrapper

Really, it is a case of knowing how to distinguish between the person speaking and what is being said, just as we are accustomed to make another distinction between the sinner and the sin. Augustine uses a very down-to-earth simile to get this idea across:

> Pay attention to what we minister . . . What should not concern you is the kind of dish in which the food you are eager to eat is offered to you . . . The dish may be silver, gold, or clay, but what you must be concerned with is whether it contains bread, whose bread it is, and whose gift it is that is being served to you [S 340A, 9].

What he is saying is an age-old truth: hungry people will not concern themselves about the kind of plate on which they get their food, be it paper or plastic, china or crystal. What they do care about is the food itself, that it be nourishing for continued growth of body and soul. Even today we are accustomed to use many such similes ourselves to remind ourselves and others to pay attention to what is important, the content, and not be caught up by what is merely superficial.

Although no one can really judge a book by its cover, there are perhaps all too many of us who are led to buy books because of an appealing title or an attractive cover. Though we shouldn't do it, is it all so uncommon to choose a package that is attractively wrapped, and pass over one with plain wrappings? In some way this reminds me of St. James' letter to the early Christians, which admonishes us precisely not to judge our fellow human beings by externals, their dress or jewelry for example [see Jas 2:1-7]. The same thing also happens today, as yesterday, regarding the Word of God. If the preacher's style is not to our liking, it is all too easy to turn him off, not to hear what he is saying, even though his content may be very good. Quite unfortunately our Catholic people may have to live with poor preachers at times. Catholics cannot fire their priests, but they can and certainly should speak up about such a situation if it becomes necessary.

Augustine himself was a victim of this mentality before his conversion: he refused to attend to what the Scriptures said because the style in which they were written (their "wrapper," so to speak) was not the Ciceronian style he had absorbed from his youth and which had been drilled into him at every level of his education. He felt it was beneath his dignity to "waste" his time on such "poorly written" material. In this way intellectual pride kept him from understanding the sacred writings for many years. And that is exactly what Augustine did not want to happen to his people, even though there was little possibility of this happening as long as they were listening to him.

Weak and Mortal

Augustine likewise did not fail to impress upon his people that their priests and bishops were very human, just like themselves—one more good reason why hope should not be placed in these ministers, but in God. How very different was this attitude of the more mature Augustine from that of the facile criticism which had marked his earlier days, before ordination. Then Augustine had found it easy to accuse other ministers of the Church of failure before he had to step into their shoes. Much as many young people today and down through the ages, he was so taken up with an overly idealistic approach to life, that he was unable to see clearly the very fact of his own mortality and weakness—and that of others!—about which later he had to speak to his people:

> And who is the person placed over you except someone just like yourself? Your pastor lives in human flesh; he is mortal. He eats, sleeps, and wakes up. He was born and he is going to die. When you think about it, he is, in himself, simply a man. But it is true that you make him something more by giving him honor; it is as if you were covering over what is weak [S 46, 6].

That last phrase, "covering over what is weak," deserves a little more attention. In former times it seems that not a few of the faithful adopted such a view concerning their priests and religious. They either chose to cloak over the failings of their priests, or they chose to forget that their priests shared a weak humanity with them. This latter tendency led some to think that, because of their high calling, priests and religious should be able to overcome or avoid the temptations and falls to which other people are subject. No wonder, then, that at times they would react with dismay when their ministers would not properly live up to the high and often varying expectations which the people had for them. On the other hand, those who hid their priests' failings, while being very much aware of their humanity, would sometimes tend to tolerate in them what they would never tolerate in others, probably not even in members of their own families: alcoholism, impropriety with the opposite sex, rudeness, and sometimes a very haughty demeanor. Such an attitude was really of no help to those priests, who perhaps could have been aided in a very positive way by a timely correction. On his own part, while Augustine expected a lot from his fellow ministers, just as he did from himself [see S 356], he did not expect the impossible. Indeed, we see how once more he tried to refocus the "honor" attributed to him so that the people would be more aware of the goodness of God and would give the honor to God:

> Therefore let us love not ourselves but him, and in feeding his sheep seek his interests and not our own, for in some inexplicable way those who love themselves instead of God do not love themselves, and those who love God and not themselves do love themselves [On John 123, 5].

I think it is worthwhile to add a few more words at this point concerning a topic barely mentioned so far: the interplay of idealism and realism. This interplay is a fact that should concern us constantly. Augustine approaches this topic at length in his commentary on Psalm 99, showing that it is easy to exaggerate the virtuous living of Christians in general, as also of the clergy and of religious. Such an exaggeration is able to attract others to these various states in life, but they come with a false picture, an extremely idealistic picture –much as Augustine himself had of certain superiors in the monasteries he had visited in Rome just after his baptism [see Customs I, 32]. And when these people meet up with reality—namely, that things are not as rosy as they were made out to be!—they become not only disappointed, but bitter, critical, cynical, even at times intolerant.

Augustine drives home here a very important lesson: all of us need to emphasize the good and the positive, but we cannot allow ourselves to lose sight of our own limitations, as well as of those of others. We cannot expect perfection in others, any more than we find it in ourselves. It is also true that idealism is an important ingredient of life: it is an interior power that keeps us moving ahead even in difficult times. It keeps our sights set high. But it also needs to be mitigated by realism: we are who we are, and so are other people. We all have our limitations. As we would like others to understand and tolerate these limitations, or even help us correct them, so must we be patient, understanding, and at times tolerant of the limitations of others, unless Christian charity obliges us to intervene in special circumstances.

It seems appropriate to mention here one of the great weaknesses Augustine experienced in his pastoral service with regard to the praise given him by others, which was plentiful. He is tremendously open in telling us of this problem, and what he has to say may be of great help to all of us in our various walks of life. For it is only natural and right that others show sincere gratitude and praise for the good things we may be able to do for them. There is nothing wrong with accepting such gratitude, as long as we keep things in perspective, and take more joy in the gift God has given us than in the gift of praise which others give us. Listen to how Augustine addresses this weakness in his *Confessions:*

> [Sometimes] a person is praised for some gift received from you, Lord. If this person takes more pleasure in the praise than in the possession of the gift for which praise is being offered, then acceptance of that praise detracts from you. In this case the person offering the praise is better off than the one receiving it. Because while that person has delighted in God's gift in another, the person who is praised has taken more delight in the gift of praise, given by a human, than in the gift itself, received from God [Conf 10, 36].

> When others come to know the words we speak and the things we do, we can be seriously tempted. In fact our love of praise can lead us to seek out this praise, in order to build up our own miserable pride. This is a temptation that sticks with me, even when my will disapproves of it. And often one will take pride in the very disapproval of such praise, which is the very height of vanity [Conf 10, 38].

Priest and People, Learning Together

Besides asking his people to be realistic about their ministers, Augustine also urges them to develop an attitude of attentive listening and obedience to the Word, which, though it reaches them from the outside, from the mouth of the preacher, is nevertheless at the same time rooted in the interior of a person's being. In this, priest and people are alike: both are obliged to give careful attention to that interior Word, and to carry it out faithfully in the way they live:

> It follows that your duty is to act, ours to make you more attentive; for you are the hearers of the Word and we are its

preachers. But within, where no one can see, we are all hearers . . . I speak from outside, he rouses you from within. All of us, then, inwardly are listeners; but outwardly, all of us in the sight of God must be doers [S 179, 7].

On us falls the duty of speaking, so as not to be judged and condemned; on you falls the duty of listening, of listening with your heart, so as not to be called to account in regard to what we give you: or better, so as to be able to show a profit and not a loss when you are so called to account [On John 12, 4, 39].

This sense of unity between priest and people, as those who are enlightened and guided mutually by the same Lord, is brought out in still other ways as Augustine stresses that all Christians are in communion with the one Lord. And as he readily acknowledges, future bishops may well come from those who are now listening to him:

You indeed belong to one household now; all of us who are stewards belong to the same household, and we all belong to one Lord. What I give you is not a gift of my own; it is from him, from whom I too receive what I need . . . For how many in this congregation are destined to be stewards? We too once stood where you are standing; we too, who are now seen distributing food to our fellow-servants from a position above them, were a few years ago receiving food with our fellow-servants down where you are. I speak as a bishop to the laity, but how do I know how many future bishops I am speaking to? [S 101, 4].

Be Bishops in Your Own Homes

Augustine also insisted that those who heard him had a duty to speak up for their faith. In other words, they could not simply receive the gift of faith and have it nourished by the bishop in a passive way; they had to share this gift with others, particularly in their own homes, but also in other places where it might be difficult for the bishop to be present. In fact Augustine says they are even to take his place, to be like bishops in their homes, because they are called to watch over the growth of the faith among those of their household:

Where Christ is censured, you must defend him: answer the grumblers, reprove the blasphemers, and avoid their company. Thus you make good use of your money if there are some people you can show as your profit. Act my part in your own homes . . . Those who are the head of a household must exercise the office of bishop in their own home and watch over the faith of their own people, so that none of them falls into heresy . . . [S 94].

The logical conclusion of all this is that it is not the bishop who is the ultimate guardian of the faith, but the Lord. I cannot read your minds or your hearts, Augustine tells them. My care for you is very weak and very human. But there is one who cares for you totally and who will help you live as God wishes: "Unless the LORD guard the city, in vain does the guard keep vigil" [Ps 127:1].

It is true that we can observe your goings and comings, but it is also true that we can not see what you are thinking in your hearts. We can not even see what you are doing in your own homes. How then are we your guardians? In a very human way: to the best of our ability, and in keeping with our talents . . . We labor at our guard duties, but our labor is in vain unless he guards you who sees your thoughts . . . I watch over you because of the office entrusted to me, but I also want to be watched over with you. I am a pastor for you, but a sheep with you under the care of the true Shepherd. From this position I am as it were a teacher for you, but I am also your fellow disciple in this school, under that one true Teacher [On Ps 126, 3].

Caring for Temporal Needs

One final topic needs to be touched here. It is Augustine's concern, not just for the spiritual well-being of his people, but also for their temporal needs. Indeed, it was his care for these temporal necessities that were the hardest for him to bear, that literally exhausted him and made him long for those better days, when he had been able to give himself more to contemplative prayer. Yet, though he complained to his friends about what this concern cost him, he kept up his efforts as long as his health permitted. It is touching and at times perhaps a bit comical to see how he addresses this subject in speaking to the people. At one moment he chides those who seem to think he is wasting his time in running to this or that government official and he pleads for their understanding. And then later, at age seventy-two, he literally begs his people to keep the agreement they had made with him publicly on an earlier occasion, namely to allow him more free time to dedicate himself to the study of the Scriptures:

> You all know that it is your own needs that compel us to go where we would rather not, to watch for the right moment, to stand in line at the door, to wait while the reputable and the disreputable alike are shown in, to get ourselves announced, to be received at long last, and then to pour our heart out in pleading, bearing in silence the humiliations heaped upon us, and for all our pains to succeed only sometimes, while other times we have to go away disgruntled [S 302, 17].

> We had agreed with one another that in view of the scriptural studies which my fathers and fellow-bishops of the two provincial synods of Carthage and Numidia had enjoined me to undertake, nobody was to disturb me for five days in the week. This was entered in the record and approved by acclamation . . . For a short while you kept to your bargain, but you have ever since most outrageously failed to keep it, for you leave me no time to do what I want to do. Both morning and afternoon, you take all my time. I beseech you most earnestly, for Christ's sake, that you will agree to my handing over all my more time-consuming tasks to this young man whom I have this day in Christ's name designated as my successor, namely the priest Eraclius [L 213, 5, cited in *Meer* 272].

This latter quote from the seventy-two-year-old bishop, begging his people's understanding about his personal need for study time, evokes striking similarities with the petition that Augustine made at age thirty-seven, just after his ordination as a priest, when he begged his bishop to free him for deeper scriptural studies. In neither case are we aware of the answer Augustine received. But it would seem that he got what he felt he needed on both occasions: more time for study and writing.

To sum up, Augustine truly loved his people, despite their sometimes trying characteristics, and they loved him. He got along with them famously, even when he had to rebuke them: they knew that even then he was on their side and would do all he could for their spiritual progress and even, at times, for their temporal good. He made them very much aware of his own weakness, of the need for a realistic approach to life, of the fact that he and they were called by the Lord to learn together and help one another grow. He highly esteemed them, and urged them to be so many other bishops— literally "overseers"—in their homes and anywhere else they could proclaim the faith by their example. Above all he requested their prayers for himself and for them, "that we may bear one another's burdens and thus fulfill the law of Christ" [see Gal 6:2]. Probably the best conclusion we can all draw for ourselves is this: Let us go and do likewise!

8

To Bear Another's Burdens, and Our Own!

Several years ago, when I was giving a retreat to Augustinian missionaries in Japan, one of the brothers made a very interesting suggestion to me. He said in so many words: "We hear a lot about the wonderful things Augustine did both as a religious and priest/bishop. But we rarely hear anything about the pastoral problems he faced or how he resolved them. It would be great if you could write something about these for our personal and pastoral encouragement. Surely this would give us some insights into our own pastoral concerns and would make Augustine's very real humanity come to life all the more for us."

This fine suggestion was on my mind for quite a few years before I was finally able to give it expression in what follows. Though originally written to satisfy that well-expressed request of our missionaries, these reflections have been included in this book basically for three reasons: first, so that we can continue our reflections on the ministerial priesthood; second, so that being more aware of some of the crosses their priests run up against, the Christian people may perhaps see their priests in a new and different light; and third, because the burdens spoken of here could also be applied to many, if not all people, in the fields of business, professional life, running a household, and in other positions of responsibility.

Augustine the priest and bishop did indeed have many pastoral concerns, just like church leaders of our own day. He was also very human, and he never ceased to remind his people of this fact, as we have seen above in chapter 7. He experienced frustration, discouragement, disappointment, and failure, as well as great joy, encouragement, hope, and success. He often spoke about these things in his sermons, or even wrote about them in his letters and books. As one good Christian I met in the Philippines put it: "It's easy for me to identify with Augustine because, like the rest of us, he began his journey at the bottom of the mountain: he had experiences like I do. He had to struggle all the way to the top; no angel just picked him up and put him there."

It is true: Augustine's journey through life was not an easy one. We have already looked at some of the problems and sufferings that were his in coming to the Catholic faith [see chapter 4]. On the other hand, not many are aware of the numerous trials and struggles he went through as a respected religious leader of his times. Looking a little more closely at these matters can perhaps give us a better appreciation, not only of Augustine's very human characteristics, but also of those of every priest and bishop. Hopefully they will also help us to understand what made Augustine a truly faithful son of the Church and of our heavenly Father. His is a great example, not only for priests and bishops, but also for the Christian people.

Augustine's Burdens

A constantly recurring word in Augustine's writings is "burden." It is a word he frequently associates with St. Paul's admonition that we should bear one another's burdens and in this manner fulfill the law of Christ, which is the law of love [see Gal 6:2]. Augustine believed this thoroughly! When he asked his people to pray that he might be able to bear his great burden as their leader, he also informed them that, in this manner, they would be doing nothing other than praying for themselves. For in reality they were his burden, and he needed their help in order to commend and carry them safely to God:

> Pray for me then that the one who did not refuse to put up with me may also deign to carry my burden with me. When you pray in this manner, you are also praying for yourselves, for what else is this burden of mine if not yourselves. Pray then that I may be strong, just as I pray that you may not be too burdensome [S 340, 1].

He advised a group of monks that they should bear with one another in love. If you cannot put up with your own brothers, he said, who will you be able to put up with? [see L 48, 3]. Furthermore, if all of us are really to help one another as Christ desires, then we must also bear one another's burdens as though they were our own. Is not that what is meant by that legendary proverb which says we should try to walk a mile in someone else's shoes before we judge that person? Love, Augustine reminds us, allows all of us to put up with any burden when we are sincerely searching for unity [see On 1 John 1, 13]. Moreover, a loving obedience offers us an opportunity to share the burden and cares of an entire community, be it a diocesan, parish, school, religious, or family community, or even a broader grouping. By such obedience or acceptance of leadership we not only show compassion toward those who are in charge, but we also promote the welfare of the entire group [see *Rule* 7]. This too represents a good example of how we can seek unity and cement it.

Though Augustine had been quite critical of some priests and bishops in his youth, he still highly esteemed the priesthood and the episcopacy, even before he took them on himself. While he was well aware that these offices could be abused by those who sought them for their own glory and not for God's, he also made it clear that these offices could bring great joy to those who fulfilled their duties well.

In his first five years as a Catholic Christian, Augustine had apparently come to know both good and bad ministers. From one of his earliest books, written as a layman a year or two after his conversion, we learn that he had been very impressed by some fine Church leaders and had deeply admired the difficult virtues they possessed and practiced. At the same time we learn what some of the burdens or crosses of these men actually were:

> How many wonderful and holy men have I known among bishops, priests, deacons and every rank of the ministers of the divine mysteries! Their virtue seems to me all the more worthy of admiration and praise considering how much harder it is to practice in the most varied circumstances and in a way of life that is anything but peaceful. Indeed, the people entrusted to them are not sound and healthy, but such as need constant care and attention. They must have patience with the moral frailty of the people in order to heal them, and before they can calm the tempest, they must bear its brunt. In such circumstances it is very difficult to maintain an exemplary conduct and keep one's spirit perfectly calm [Customs I, 32, 69].

Much as we might like the idea, we simply do not live in a sin-free Church; the members of Christ are still burdened by sin and the temptation to sin. There will always be those who are drawn all too easily to some of the unchristian attractions that pervade our society, and who as a result are in special need of pastoral care and concern. Priests and ministers need much patience today, as in Augustine's time. They also need to pray in a special way for the grace to keep their own personal conduct above those fatal attractions which could cause them to lose their effectiveness with the very people they are trying to serve.

In what follows I would like to take a look at five specific areas of life in which Augustine experienced first-hand particular burdens or crosses, some more troublesome, some less. As should be clear, these burdens are not limited to ministers. Any of us can and probably do experience one or the other or even all of them at some stage in our lives.

The Burden of Ministry

The first burden that faces any religious, priest, or bishop is that of providing a ministry that is in keeping with what the Lord asks of all who serve in the Church. Yet strangely enough, though this very ministry is quite a burden at times, it is also the greatest source of one's happiness and joy, when carried out to the best of one's ability. It is for this very reason that Augustine frequently commends his ministry to his people, hoping to help them recognize that he must render an account to God, not only for himself, but also for them. This will once again turn his burden into joy:

> [M]y burden is much greater, but if it is carried well it will bring about a greater glory; if it is borne unfaithfully, however, it will cast us down to a horrendous punishment. What is therefore the most important thing I should do today, except to commend my danger to you, so that you might be my joy? [S 339, 1]

But what are some of the specific pastoral burdens that Augustine encounters? On several occasions he tells us how much he misses the more contemplative lifestyle he was leading before his ordination. And he goes on to say: There is nothing better or more delightful than to have quiet time for such contemplative prayer. But correcting, rebuking, and just being concerned about everybody else's welfare were a great burden and fatigue for him. "Who would not run away from such a labor," he asks [see S 339, 4]? In his *Confessions* [10, 43] Augustine implies that he felt so weighed down by his sins and his personal inadequacy that he was half-determined to do just that—run away from his duties. But the Lord made it clear that he should stick to his ministry, difficult though he found it, and that is what he did:

> I am speaking on orders from the Lord; I cannot be silent, for he strikes terror into me. Who would not prefer to be silent and not to have to give an account of you? But the fact remains that we have been saddled with a burden that we cannot and must not shake off our shoulders [S 82, 15].

Is this not applicable to anyone in a position of responsibility even today?

The Burden of Correcting Others

Augustine was particularly reluctant about having to decide whether a person was to be corrected or punished, and if so how this should be done. He saw clearly the need for some disciplinary measures at times, but all was to be done in the spirit of love and with gentleness. Yet he agonized over such decisions, as becomes evident in a letter addressed to his good friend Paulinus:

> How much can a person stand? Are there not punishments a person will balk at, such that not only will he derive no advantage from them, but he will also collapse under their severity? What deep dark questions! . . . I do not know either how many people have become better because of punishment or how many have turned out worse on its account. And what is one to do in the case that frequently presents itself: If you punish a certain person, he is lost; if you allow his wrongdoing to go unchecked, another person is corrupted by it? [L 95, 3]

From my own experience I know the mental agony Augustine was talking about here. I have felt that crushing burden in the sacrament of reconciliation when having to refuse absolution to those very few who were evidently not really sorry for their sins or were unwilling to try to change. I have lived it as a superior in the religious life, who had to intervene or try to settle occasional disputes among brothers, or between them and their superiors. Even as headmaster of a school, I have agonized over the same dilemma Augustine speaks of. What is really best for a person or a particular situation: correction or silence?

The Burden of Pride and Ignorance

Possidius, Augustine's friend and first biographer, tells us that Augustine wept at his ordination because he foresaw the very real burdens that this ministry would impose on him [Possidius 4]. Possidius calls these burdens "dangers," but the idea is the same. Augustine remembered how as a layman he had rashly and proudly criticized some ministers, and now he feared falling into these very ministerial errors himself. He feared a return to that pride which had done him in for so many years in his early manhood. He recognized that he still did not know enough about the Scriptures and was concerned about how he could best communicate them to others who now, after his ordination, depended on him. Because he was so anxious to correct this situation, he wrote to his bishop in this fashion:

> When I was put in this position, I realized the recklessness of my former complaints, although it is true that even then I considered this to be a very dangerous ministry . . . Now I have experienced even greater and more extensive difficulties than those I had previously imagined. Not because I have discovered new waves or unknown storms . . . but because I was ignorant of my own power and wisdom to calm the storm or confront it. I had not realized what nimble diligence was needed to steer clear of these waves or storms, or to brave them. I did not know my own powers, and I held them to be considerable [L 21, 2].

What Augustine tells us is what every Christian, ministers included, must be aware of: Do not overestimate your strength! Do not try to do everything by yourself. No one can bear the burdens of ministry or other heavy responsibilities without a lot of prayer and study, without "asking, seeking, knocking" at the Father's door in order to receive real counsel:

> There may be—indeed there certainly are—written in the holy books, counsels that the man of God must know thoroughly . . . But how can he get to know these counsels, except as the Lord has told us: by asking, seeking, knocking [Matt 7:7; Luke 11:9], that is, by prayer, by study, by tearful supplication? [L 21, 4]

It is so easy for priests to get wrapped up in their own success as teachers, preachers, counselors, healers, or even as effective writers or communicators. It takes tremendous humility to recognize that real success in serving others is principally God's doing. God works through his ministers, using their strengths and weaknesses, many or few as they may be, just as he did with his prophets and his first disciples. Nevertheless, they, like others, can easily come to believe that it is they who are essential, not the Lord. Or that the Lord can only accomplish his works through them. It may be hard to understand, but at times even the weaknesses of priests can help bring others to Christ.

The Burden of Not Having Enough Time for Oneself

Augustine's need for searching the Scriptures leads us to another burden that weighed on him, one that almost everyone can easily identify with today: *he had no real time for himself.* His time was almost totally given over to the people, so much so that he frequently had only a few night hours to himself for meditative prayer and writing. For many he was a respected "judge" of their disputes, just as Moses had been for the Israelites. And we can well remember how this literally exhausted Moses, until his phantom father-in-law came on the scene [just one brief scene!] and gave him some excellent advice about sharing the burden among others, especially in what involved lesser decisions. For others Augustine was the one to plead their cases before civil servants, often suffering humiliation at their hands.

People came to him for all kinds of advice, even seeking his blessing or approval [if we can believe it!] in immoral matters:

> Sometimes their manner of living is such that they come to the bishop or seek his advice on how to rob someone of his possessions. I speak from experience, because this has actually happened to me; otherwise I wouldn't believe it myself. Many seek evil advice from me, advice on lying and cheating, on how to subtly deceive others, thinking to please me. But I assure you in Christ's name . . . no such people have found in me what they were looking for [S 137, 14].

What a terrible burden for any minister to have to warn the people about such things! Augustine was so given over to helping his own people—and those of other faiths as well!— that he would sometimes go without eating the entire day rather than stop receiving them. Most important of all for him was the spiritual good of his people:

> [H]e always examined the facts and passed judgment with an eye on the movements of Christian souls, that is, considering how each party was advancing or falling off in faith and morals. He took the opportunity of teaching both parties the truth of God's law and bringing it home to them and of reminding them of the means of obtaining eternal life [Possidius 19, 3-4].

On one occasion he wrote to a friend, Marcellinus by name, telling him how very busy he was kept:

> If I were to give you an account of how the hours of my days and nights are spent, and let you see how many of them I have to spend over unnecessary things, it would make you quite sad; you would also be astonished at the number of things which I cannot put off and which pluck me by the sleeve and prevent me from doing what you are questioning and begging me about—the things which I would so gladly do myself, but which, to my unspeakable regret, I am not in a position to do [L 139, 3].

This same thought was uppermost in his mind when he wrote to Abbot Eudoxius, begging him and his fellow monks to offer special prayers for him: "For we believe that you pray very alertly and attentively, whereas our own prayers are weighed down and weakened by the darkness and confusion that secular involvement brings with it . . . We are beset by so many problems that we can hardly breathe" [L 48, 1].

Once again we can see hidden under this appeal a tremendous desire to return to a more contemplative lifestyle, to be free of the many administrative burdens [that "secular involvement"] which the office of bishop brought with it in those days, such as administering justice, pleading especially for the weak and the young, caring for the Church's material goods, providing materially for the poor and the suffering. In Augustine's own case there were also the innumerable appeals of other bishops, priests, and laity to write in defense of the young church or in defense of this or that teaching of the Church, especially against those then very appealing errors which were being promoted by the Donatists, the Aryans, and the Pelagians.

The Burden of Poor Health

It is really remarkable that Augustine did not suffer that very common and most debilitating illness of our own times: *burnout!* On the other hand, maybe he did! Just after his conversion, during the early part of his stay in Cassaciacum [a country place, about thirty-five miles north of Milan], he went through a crisis which has all the earmarks of extreme tension, which can easily lead to burnout [see Conf 9, 2]. Yet he not only survived; he actually thrived in his generous service to others, despite a chronically weak physical constitution, which was surely another heavy burden for him. In the light of the many physical, mental, and psychological ills that can and do afflict people in positions of responsibility today, it might be a good thing to reflect a little more on Augustine's own difficulties in this regard, if for no other reason than to encourage others in their own, at times overwhelming, tasks of ministry or service.

We get some hint of Augustine's physical weaknesses in his *Confessions*. There, from early childhood, we find him frequently susceptible to serious illnesses, the kind that twice brought him close to death's door: at six or seven years of age or thereabouts, and again at about twenty-eight. As Father Trapè points out in his excellent work on Augustine:

> It was not any "indisposition of the mind" but "weak health" that kept him from journeys on and across the sea, which his brother bishops undertook for the sake of their ministry. He could not stand the cold; he was tortured by "the pain and swelling of hemorrhoids" that often kept him abed; his voice was so weak that he could not be heard unless there was complete silence; more than once while speaking he confessed to weakness and a failing voice [Trapè, 30–31].

Though his mind remained perfectly sharp till the very end of his life, he had to adapt himself to the limitations of his body from a very early time. Yet even these afore-mentioned limitations did not keep him from making what, for those times, must have been considered quite long land journeys. He was a frequent visitor to Carthage [bordering on Tunis in modern-day Tunisia], where the patriarch of the region presided and where Augustine gave some of his finest sermons. This amounted to about a four-hundred-mile round trip, over a rough road, in a most uncomfortable carriage or on horseback. When he was sixty-four, upon the insistence of Pope Zosimus, he undertook a thousand-mile journey from Hippo to Carthage and on to Caesarea in Mauretania and back to Hippo [see Trapè, 253]. Especially in the light of his known difficulties, we cannot help but marvel at the physical stamina of this servant of God, not to mention his intellectual prowess. So many of us today seem to lack the staying power of such a giant as Augustine. Yet, though we may not be able to imitate him in many ways, perhaps we can imitate him in what drove him to give his all, with generosity. "Love and do what you will," he told the people [On 1 John 7, 8]. It was what he practiced himself to the highest degree.

Other Burdens and Joys

We have reflected on some of Augustine's burdens in providing spiritual leadership for his people. There were certainly many others, for example, the early divided community, Catholic and Donatist; the indifference of so many who came to church only to be seen or to see others [something Augustine had done himself in his early college days in Carthage as we read in *Confessions* 3, 4]; people who drank too much and fairly wallowed in the passionate drama of the theaters; problems with refugees pouring in from Italy to escape the Barbarian invasions. It sounds very much like some of our modern-day problems.

There were these and many other burdens to be carried, because for Augustine presiding over a community meant being useful to others and putting up with these crosses. At the same time, however, there were also many joys associated with that ministry. There was nothing more joyful for him than a generous pastoral service of others [L 21, 1]. He took great pleasure in speaking of the things of God, both in public and in private conversation [Possidius 19, 6]. Giving alms to the poor is the way to fill up one's treasure house. Augustine did this, both by preaching and by sharing his food with his fellow-poor, even to melting down chalices to provide for them [see S 376A, 3; also S 339]. Learning about the gentle and humble Christ leads us to faith, hope, and love [see S 164, 7]. And the practice of faith, as well as faith itself, gives us a sure consolation in the face of death [see City 19, 8].

Though from time to time Augustine complained of his burdens, it was never in a spirit of bitterness, but rather in the spirit of a servant who feels overwhelmed by his responsibilities, perhaps like Jeremiah. Yet through all this his trust in the Lord knew no bounds: he was confident that God would make up for his own imperfections, that his weakness would be more than compensated by the strength of Christ working in and through him. That trust and confidence grew through an ever deepening prayer life. I firmly believe that is the way it is with many of us who are struggling to continue growing in our faith today.

These considerations remind all of us that matters will not always be as peaceful or harmonious as we would like them to be. There will be rough periods in our lives, and these will try our patience, our humility, our true dedication to our work, no matter what that work may be. At times we ourselves will be the cause of our own problems: through poor judgment, or insensitivity to the needs of others, or lack of understanding of our own limitations. At times our burdens will come from others who are proud and adamant in their ways, or expect too much of us, or who are always finding fault, no matter what we do. But through it all we need to be gratefully aware that God will not let us down, and that if we are open to his workings in us, God can and will accomplish great things through us for others.

9

Building the City of God

What does the Church mean to you? Is it only the place where you gather for worship? Is it the hierarchy, those who lead the Church: pope and bishops, and maybe priests? Is it all the baptized? Is it limited by natural or national boundaries: the church of Spain, of the United States, of Italy, of Mexico?

For Augustine the Church was more than any of these. It was the Whole Christ, in other words it is Jesus the Head, joined to the body of all the baptized. There was no question in his mind that the Church was universal; it was certainly not limited by the boundaries of North Africa as the Donatists held, nor was it limited by any other natural or national boundaries. The Whole Christ could never have such limits [see S 213, 8].

The Church as Mother

As Augustine sees it, the Church is indeed our mother—she gives us birth in the Spirit so that we might attain eternal life [see L 243, 8]. On the other hand, the members of the Church show that they possess this Spirit by the love they manifest for peace, unity, and the Church itself [see On 1 John 6, 10], and they go on loving the Church as long as they stand fast in her membership and loving embrace [see On John 32, 8].

Augustine provides us with a marvelous description of the extent of mother Church's love for each and every one of us, which it is well worth our while to reflect on:

> See what [this mother] has given you: she has united the creature to its Creator, she has made sons and daughters of God of those who were servants, she has made brothers and sisters of Christ those who were slaves of the devil. You will not be ungrateful for so many great blessings if you offer her the respectful courtesy of your presence. No one can enjoy the favor of God the Father if they look down on mother Church. This holy and spiritual mother prepares spiritual nourishment for you every day, by which to strengthen, not your bodies, but your souls. The Church grants you the bread from heaven and gives you to drink the chalice of salvation. The Church does not want any of her children to suffer hunger for lack of these foods. For your own good, my very dear children, do not abandon a mother like this, so that you may be filled with the abundance of her house . . . After having nourished you faithfully, may she lead you free and healthy to the eternal fatherland [S 255A].

Though rather lengthy, this quotation reveals a lot of the love Augustine himself felt for mother Church, that Church to which he had returned only after a long and painful journey, which at one point had almost led him to despair. This quote is an appeal to all the faithful to honor the Church as God the Father does, to be grateful for her many gifts and nourishment on our journey through life, and to remain faithful to her so that she can fully accomplish her mission of leading us to our eternal home.

The Church as Community

But though the Church is our mother, the Church is also a community. One of Augustine's most famous works, *The City of God*, reveals this broader view of the Church as the city of God here on earth. This city, or better, this community, is made up of all those who live by the Spirit, who are rooted in the love of God, who seek to serve one another, who find their strength in God, who worship God alone and strive for the same goal of holiness and happiness in God.

This community stands in stark contrast to that other community or society which also has its existence among us, which Augustine calls the city of the world.

Those who belong to this worldly city or community are rooted, not in the love of God, but in the love of self. They live only for the purpose of satisfying the desires of the flesh, seek to dominate others, trust only in their own skills and strength and are convinced they can get along by themselves without outside help, either from God or from anyone else [see City 14, 28]. While we must be very careful not to proclaim ourselves as better than others, as the Pharisee did regarding the tax collector in the Gospel [see Luke 18:9-14], we cannot help but realize that this picture of two contrasting communities is also verified in our own times.

There must be no mistaking where our sympathies lie, where our strength is rooted, what community we belong to. It ought to be very clear to us that we cannot hope to make the journey to God or achieve our final destiny by ourselves. If we are to persevere in our calling as Christians, we are all very much in need of the cohesive strength of that community's love, of the support of our brothers and sisters, of the need to share solid Christian values with one another, and of the witness and encouragement of the good lives of others. Even though people who believe in Christ may be gathered together in one place, even if it be a church, for example, "they do not constitute a house of the Lord until they are joined together by love" [S 336, 1–2]. Simply being together in the same place is no guarantee that we are really a temple of the Lord; only love for one another provides the necessary proof that we really are that temple.

Augustine compares the building up of the Christian community to the building of a church: no one is going to want to enter that church or take part in its worship unless the stones and the beams that make it up are firmly held together and there is no danger of collapse. Much less will people want to join with us in worship, that is, form one community with us, if they see that there is nothing firmly holding us together, or what is worse, that we are divided, disrespectful, or unsupportive of one another. In other words, they will not be encouraged or attracted to us unless they see that we are a healthy community, where unity and love prevail:

> The very health of this body [the Church] exists in the unity of the members and in their bond of love. If anyone's love should grow cold, that person is sick in the body of Christ. But the One who raised up Jesus our Head is able to heal our sick members, provided, that is, that they have not cut themselves off from the body, but cling to it until they are healed [S 137, 1].

Is not the same true of a school or parish community? Where teachers and students, priests and people are firmly united in the task at hand, where there is mutual respect and support, the very healthfulness and firmness of the community will always attract others to join them.

Augustine speaks eloquently of the power of love. He makes clear, as does St. Paul in 1 Corinthians 13, that love is the only thing that really counts, the only thing that is lasting, and most important of all, the only thing that distinguishes the members of God's community from those who belong to the worldly community:

> Love is the only real distinction between the children of God and the children of the devil. All may sign themselves with the sign of Christ's cross, answer Amen and sing Alleluia. All may be baptized, come to church and line the walls of our meeting places. There is nothing to distinguish the children of God from the children of the devil except love . . . You may have whatever else you will, but if this one thing is lacking to you, nothing else will help you. If you lack all the rest and have love, you have fulfilled the law [On 1 John 5, 7].

> You say that you love Christ? Keep his commandment and love your brothers and sisters. But if you do not love them, how can you be said to love him whose commandment you actually despise? Brothers and sisters, I am never satisfied, never finished, in speaking of love in the name of the Lord . . . Let us hold to the unity of the Church, hold to Christ, hold to love. Let us not be pulled away from any of the members of his spouse, the Church, not be torn away from faith, that we may glory in his coming [On 1 John 9, 11].

The Early Church Community as a Model

In his sermons and writings Augustine frequently referred to the early Christian community of Jerusalem as a model for other communities. He was particularly impressed by what the Acts of the Apostles said of the members of this community: that they were "of one heart and one mind" [Acts 4:32]. In his early days as a Christian and priest, Augustine interpreted this passage as though the "one mind and one heart" referred to each individual person as being single-hearted and undivided in themselves. Later on he applied this saying, not just to individuals, but also to entire communities, telling them that, though they were made up of many people, they should really be of only one heart and mind on the way to God: "They are many bodies, but not many souls; many bodies, but not many hearts" [On Ps 132, 6]. This very same idea, which has constituted the ideal of Augustine's religious communities since the fourth century, was also applied by Augustine to the entire community of believers. By extension it can also be applied to school and parish communities if they are really communities of faith and love:

> All believers together form one single place for the Lord. For the Lord finds his place in the human heart, because when many people are bound to one another in love they have but one heart. Many thousands of people put their faith into practice by laying the proceeds of their goods at the feet of the apostles. And what does Scripture say of them? They became the temple of God. Not only did each of them individually become the temple of God, but all of them together. They all became a sacred place for the Lord. And so that you might realize that in that whole multitude but one single place for the Lord has been made, Scripture says: "They were of one mind and one heart" on the way to God [On Ps 131, 4-5].

The Power of Example

Now all this has evident implications for our lives as members of the various families or communities we belong to: the home family, the parish family, the school family, in my case the Augustinian family, or wherever else we are closely joined with others by ties of faith and love. If we are really a community in the Lord, if the Lord has truly chosen us as his temple, both individually and along with other like-spirited people, then we can no longer be exclusively concerned for our own personal interests. We must necessarily have the interests of others at heart also, particularly those of the Christian community.

For example, Augustine considers the family a mini-Church, a small cell which has need of direction and encouragement in the faith, just as the entire Church does on a broader scale [see S 94]. Who can best give that direction and encouragement? Certainly not the bishop or the local priest; their duties take them in entirely different directions. Nor can the local Catholic school or parish adequately supply for this need with regard to growing children—though believe me, there are those who would love to fix much of the responsibility on teachers and pastors. No, the real responsibility lies with those in charge of the family, that is, with parents. The gift of faith that has been given to us must also be shared with others, for that is also the meaning of being a committed Christian leader. Listen to what Augustine says to his people:

> We bishops are dispensers of God's gifts: we hand over these gifts to you and you receive them. The reward that we seek is that you live good lives . . . But don't think that you yourselves are thereby exempt from making your contribution. You cannot preach from this pulpit, but you can contribute wherever else you find yourselves [S 94].

> You know how God gives the opportunity, how he opens the door with his Word. Do not stop winning others for Christ, since you yourselves have been won over by Christ [On John 10, 9].

Perhaps it is clear already, but let me emphasize it once more: the building up of community among people is a very important motif in Augustine's spirituality. The desire for greater communication and more meaningful human relationships has never been stronger than in our own times. And we would do well to take full advantage of this phenomenon. One of the great joys of belonging to the Church lies in the fact that we do form a great community with peoples of all nations and races and cultures, that we do have a very common bond, a common goal in life, and common means at hand for attaining this goal. We cannot let ourselves be unduly discouraged, much less depressed, because every now and then we meet up with some Christians who are not actually trying to live the life to which they have been called by the love of God. What we can and must do is pray for them and try to be a sign of hope for them for a better future. I guess the basic question is this: Are we sharing this hope which we enjoy with those who look to us for an example? Are we seeking to broaden their horizons?

As a result of Vatican II, we ought to understand better than ever that we are all responsible for the well-being of our Church. No one can be excused from this responsibility. We need to realize that *we* are the Church, that *we* have ownership in the Church just as the Council indicated. And because of this we must take an active part in our parishes and schools and in the role of the Church in the world we live in. Even in his own time Augustine warned his people about being merely passive members of the Church. To get this point across and to impress upon the people their personal need to be concerned and to act, he often used the image of the Church as a ship on the high seas, battered by the waves and elements:

> We are all in the same boat. Some are crew, the others are passengers. But all are in danger from the storm and all will be saved by reaching port . . . Sometimes all human advice fails us. No matter where we turn the wind roars, the storm rages, our strength faints away . . . What more can we do? This: "They cried to the Lord in their distress and from their straits he rescued them" [On Ps 106, 12].

> You must not stop praying, because you will be the first to suffer from a shipwreck. Nor should you be less concerned, nor grow tired of praying for us. You may not be at the helm, my brothers and sisters, but that doesn't mean you are not sailing on the same ship, does it? [On Ps 106, 7].

In other words, Augustine is saying you and I are in this together. Even though I may not personally experience the seriousness of the dangers to the Church as the captain of the ship does, I may well go down with him if he fails to come through. My faith is at stake, as well as my eternal salvation. I have every right to be concerned about resisting those who attack the Church. To do this I must make the best use possible of my own talents and support the efforts of those who have been given the chief responsibility in leading the Church through these difficult times in which we live.

Seeking Unity in a Divided Church

One of the greatest crosses Augustine had to bear in his earliest years as a bishop was precisely the fact that the Church of Christ was terribly divided: the Donatist schism in North Africa had wreaked havoc on the body of Christ [see chapter 1 for more on this schism]. It is no wonder, then, that a principal part of his message to the faithful and to all who would listen was directed toward achieving that long lost unity: unity in faith and unity in love. He was convinced that even one who performs miracles amounts to nothing if separated from the unity of the body of Christ [see On John 13, 17]. "How can anyone who has left the Church remain in Christ, since he is no longer among the members of Christ? How can anyone be in Christ, if he is not also in the body of Christ?" [On 1 John 1, 12].

According to Augustine, we cannot even enjoy the presence of the Holy Spirit in our lives unless we love the Church, and we will only love the Church if we remain united with her in the unity of charity [see On John 32, 7-8]. "The faithful acknowledge the body of Christ, if they do not neglect to be the body of Christ. If they want to live by the Spirit of Christ, let them become the body of Christ. Only the body of Christ lives by the Spirit of Christ . . ." [On John 26, 13].

It is interesting to see how Augustine makes love of the Church take on very human proportions as he tells his people that their love for the Church should be like love for their parents, only greater: "Love your father, then, but not more than your God. Love your mother, but not more than the

Church, which has given you birth into eternal life. Finally, as you consider the love due your parents, realize how much you should love God and the Church" [S 344, 2].

The Call to Service in the Church

This brings us to a final consideration of the Church as community: the need to engage actively in the apostolate, the need to serve others, not just in our own homes, but wherever we can. And the reason is clear, as Augustine sees it: "We must put the needs of the Church before the needs of this passing life" [L 84, 1]. We cannot remain indifferent to the needs of this very special mother, who through baptism and the Eucharist has given us a share in eternal life [see L 243, 8]. As some dedicated people—mom, dad, teachers, relatives, friends—have communicated the faith to us, made it possible for us to be healthy members of the Whole Christ, so must we be encouraged to make this possible for still others.

It is quite possible that many of us would not want to stand in a pulpit and preach, even if the Church allowed us. It is also quite possible that we would not know how to write an article or a book, or even have the time to do this. But whether for better or for worse, we can and we do preach Christ by the way we live our lives, and this is often the only way other people ever have the chance to meet the human Christ: in and through us! God forbid that the Christ they meet through us should not be the real Christ, the compassionate and loving Christ of the Gospels! Augustine sums up what all of us are capable of in a very succinct statement: "Preach Christ wherever you can, to whomever you can, and in whatever way you can. Faith is demanded of you, not eloquence. . ." [S 260 E, 2].

When Peter found himself on Mount Tabor in the presence of the glorified Christ, he did not really know what to make of it all. But he was apparently so happy to be there that he wanted to "set up tents" and remain for quite some time. In fact the implication is that he would have been happy to spend the rest of his days with Christ in glory on that mountain. I guess we would all like something similar, but that is not our life, that is not the reality we know. And

Augustine reminds Peter—and the rest of us listening in on this little conversation!—of that fact in this rather strong statement:

> Peter was tired of the crowd; he had discovered the solitude of the mountain. There he had Christ for himself . . . Why should he go back down to toil and sorrow, since he was finding there in God holy affection and therefore a happy life? . . . Go down, Peter! You wanted to rest on the mountain, but no, go down and preach the word. Stay with your task, whether you like it or not. Correct, appeal, reprove, teach at all times. Work and sweat, putting up with your share of affliction . . . To live with Christ on the mountain, Peter, is held in reserve for you after death . . . Life itself came down to meet death, bread came down to go hungry . . . and would you refuse to work? Do not seek your own advantage. Have love and preach the truth. Then you will reach eternity, where you will find security [S 78, 3; 6].

Sometimes we find ourselves in similar situations, and maybe not for the most part because of spiritual motives: we are tired and exhausted, and we wonder if what we are doing is worthwhile. And then we get a reprieve, as it were. One or the other of those we are reaching out to gives us a real lift, reminding us of how much we mean to them, what an influence for good we have been for them. How wonderful if we could keep that feeling all the time, just like Peter wanted to do. Yet we know better. That is not the way things are. We need to continue giving ourselves to this community that is the Church. There are many others in our society who very much depend on the dedication of Christians who are truly committed to their faith. As St. Paul puts it, all our talents have been given to us, not just for ourselves, but also for the good of the community. And surely the Christian leader's apostolate of concern for the developing members of our society is a concrete living out of that "bearing one another's burdens," which allows us to be loving people like Jesus.

Thank God for the Church! Thank God that we have been called as members of this spouse of Jesus Christ, who is at the same time our spiritual mother and the living body of our Savior. The Church is truly the community of God on earth, the community of those called to live with God and love him, both here and hereafter. In Augustine's words: "Let us all with complete agreement cling to God as our Father and to the Church as our mother" [On Ps 88: S 2, 14].

As a fitting conclusion to these reflections I would like to quote from an Easter sermon by Augustine that is truly a joy-filled and encouraging reflection on our faith. It has to do with the singing of the Alleluia while we are still on our journey on earth. Though some of us may not be able to sing well, there is no one of us who cannot sing as Augustine describes, for his song is a song of the heart, before it reaches our lips:

> Let us sing alleluia here on earth, while we still live in anxiety, so that we may sing it one day in heaven in full security . . . O the happiness of the heavenly alleluia, sung in security, without fear of adversity! We shall have no enemies in heaven, we shall never lose a friend . . . So then my brothers and sisters, let us sing now, not in order to enjoy a life of leisure, but in order to lighten our labors. You should sing as travelers do—sing, but continue on with your journey. Do not be lazy, but sing to make your journey more enjoyable. Sing, but keep going . . . Keep making progress [S 256, 3].